creating calm

meditation in daily life

*For Ven. Geshe Namgyal Wangchen, whose
wisdom illuminated the way*

creating calm

meditation **in daily life**

Gill Farrer-Halls

BARRON'S

Creating Calm
Gill Farrer-Halls

First published in the United States of America in 2002
by Barron's Educational Series, Inc.
First published in Great Britain in 2002 by Mitchell Beazley,
under the title *Creating Calm*, an imprint of Octopus Publishing Group Ltd.
2-4 Heron Quays, Docklands, London E14 4JP

All inquiries should be addressed to:
Barron's Educational Series, Inc.
250 Wireless Boulevard
Hauppauge, New York 11788
http://www.barronseduc.com

Library of Congress Catalog Card No.: 2001034570
International Standard Book No.: 0-7641-1921-4

Library of Congress Cataloging-in-Publication Data
Farrer-Halls, Gill.
    Creating calm : meditation in daily life / Gill Farrer-Halls.
        p. cm.
    Includes bibliographical references and index.
    ISBN 0-7641-1921-4
    1. Meditation.   I. Title.

BL627.F37   2002
291.4'35—dc21   2001034570

Printed and bound by Toppan Printing Company in China
9 8 7 6 5 4 3 2 1

contents

introduction

We would probably all like more peace and calm in our daily lives. Our modern lifestyles provide varied and interesting work together with a wide range of leisure activities, but there is a hidden price to pay. You may even have a fulfilling career and active social life, but unhealthy tensions can lie just beneath the surface. Looking deeper may reveal stress, tiredness, and a sense, which cannot easily be put into words, that all is not quite right with your life.

We are usually too busy managing our many day-to-day activities to take time out to explore this sense of unease. Understandably, the common response is to rationalize the disquieting feelings away by saying, "I need to pull myself together," "I'm lucky to have my job," "This isn't something that next year's two-week vacation won't solve." But in the midst of rushing from one thing to the next, many continue to be plagued by the persistent thought that something is amiss. Until we decide to make time to explore this feeling and find a way to make changes, peace and calm will remain elusive.

Creating Calm is designed to help you explore your inner feelings. This book offers an alternative approach to life, one that will help you to discover an inner calm. The decision to pick up this book and try out ways to create calm may be a radical one, a departure from safe familiarity. Yet the techniques and exercises suggested have been used by people the world over to find the same calm you may be hoping to find. They have been proven to work and have endured through the centuries.

The basis of all the techniques in *Creating Calm* is meditation. The word "meditation" may conjure up all sorts of associations: the image of a monk sitting cross-legged in a cave, a monastery wreathed in mist on top of a mountain, the sound of wind chimes or sonorous chants drifting on the breeze. These might create the illusion that meditation is ancient, foreign, esoteric, and therefore unsuitable or impractical for Western urban lifestyles. But meditation is not rooted in the past or in any one culture and is available and accessible to everyone here and now.

The only requirements for meditation are an open mind, the willingness to try, and the commitment to stick with it and not give up after one or two sessions. It also takes the firm resolve to find the time to meditate, which will inevitably come at the expense of something else. Meditation is not a quick-fix solution to finding peace; it requires consistent effort over time to create calm. But as the old saying goes, "if a thing is worth doing, it's worth doing well," and the benefits of meditation make the effort worthwhile.

There are descriptions, advice, and instructions for the different meditations in *Creating Calm*. In this way the book is informative, accessible, and practical, and requires no previous knowledge of meditation. Sometimes it is hard to be a beginner in our society where knowledge and expertise are valued over an open mind and the willingness to try something new. The Buddhist saying "Zen mind, Beginner's mind" is a reminder that in some ways everyone is a beginner each time a meditation session is started, even if we have done it many times before.

In keeping with different people's dispositions, different meditations suit different personalities. Some of the meditations have religious associations, others involve movement; some require creative effort, others are simple sitting; some are formal, others can be practiced in the middle of everyday life. But there is something here for everyone that could transform the mad rush of everyday life into peace and calm.

principles of meditation

essentials
of meditation

Meditation has been an essential part of life for many people from a variety of cultures since ancient times. We might think meditation is practiced only by Buddhist monks, Hindu saddhus (holy men), and Christian hermits, but these are only the most conspicuous examples. The farmer quietly watering his crops in the early light of dawn and the woman slowly walking with a pot of water on her head are equally strong archetypal images of meditation, even though we might call their actions reflection or contemplation.

meditation is an internal process of
becoming familiar with our mind and
discovering its true nature — what it is
beyond the myriad thoughts that seem to
continuously tumble through it

experiential knowledge

There are many different forms of meditation, and the word itself has several meanings. Being conscious, centered, and focused; having single-pointed concentration and clarity; being mindful, being grounded in the here and now – all these point toward the inner space experienced in meditation. We might wonder why there are several different ways to describe meditation, why there isn't one simple definition. This is because knowledge of meditation is experiential; we cannot truly know for ourselves until we try it. Only then, through our own experience, do these diverse descriptions come to life, helping us to appreciate the subtle differences between them.

who can meditate?

Meditation is not limited to those who are religious; anyone can meditate and discover the benefits without having to go to a church, synagogue, mosque, or temple each week. Meditation is an internal process of becoming familiar with our mind and discovering its true nature – what it is beyond the myriad thoughts that seem to continuously tumble through it. There is nothing about simple meditations, like mindfulness of breathing, that requires adherence to a religion, though the advice and support of a teacher and like-minded friends is most helpful. So there is no need to join any religious "club" to meditate unless we want to. However, meditation is firmly rooted in the major world religions and cannot be meaningful if divorced from the ethical guidelines the various religions espouse. Concepts such as not killing, not taking that which does not belong to us, and being truthful are common to all religions. Meditating within such an ethical framework guides us to our own inner sense of right and wrong.

setting an example

All the major figures and saints of the different religions spent time meditating, in contemplation, and in silent prayer. These experiences sometimes led to profound results, such as when Jesus went into the desert and overcame the temptations of Satan, and when Shakyamuni Buddha sat under a tree and became enlightened. Sometimes just the frequency and regularity of meditation, making it integral to daily life, brought wisdom and self-awareness to the many great sages sitting quietly in caves, on the side of riverbanks, and in churches and temples around the world.

finding such a teacher to guide us is good,
but ultimately the greatest teacher is
our own inner wisdom

inner wisdom

People are attracted to religious and spiritual teachers, who inspire those around them by their behavior. The greatest teachings are often unspoken but can be seen in a person's actions, treatment of others, and attitude. Teachers, priests, and saints who live in such a way are humble but powerful. They have attained self-awareness and profound wisdom through their meditation, prayer, and other spiritual practices. Finding such a teacher to guide us is good, but ultimately the greatest teacher is our own inner wisdom. Practicing meditation sincerely and frequently will help us awaken and develop this wisdom within. When we connect with this source of spiritual strength inside ourselves, we discover a powerful method to help us transform suffering and distress into peace and calm.

what is meditation?

Meditation can mean different things to different people, especially those from different traditions and cultures. There are a variety of meditation forms and these can be divided into two primary types: those that are done sitting without movement, and those that involve some kind of movement. One is not better than another and we may find that different methods work better for us at different times. Or, after some experimentation, we may find one technique that really works for us, and decide to stay with that meditation practice until we know it intimately and can fully realize the benefits.

All meditations share certain features. The Tibetan word for meditation, *sgom*, means to become familiar with. So meditation is a practice that requires continual effort and that must be done regularly and often to have an effect. If we practice meditation only occasionally or try it once and give up because it doesn't bring enlightenment immediately, we will not have the opportunity to become familiar with anything, except perhaps our fascination with the endless search for what is new and exciting.

The question is, what are we supposed to become familiar with? One answer is the particular meditation we have chosen to practice. If this is a sitting practice, then familiarity also refers to our mind and the contents of our mind. This may sound strange because we think we use our mind all the time and are therefore familiar with it, but actually we spend most of our time caught up in fantasies, the past and future, and following whatever line of thought pops into our head at any time. Or we engage in the study of a subject that is external, and although this requires a similar level of concentration to meditation, we do not learn much about the nature of our mind. These things – fantasies, thoughts, study – are not the mind. They are simply the contents of the mind, a surprisingly big difference. With meditation we try to go deeper and discover the nature of our mind beyond the many things tumbling through it.

practicing sitting meditation

There are two main methods of sitting meditation: calm, single-pointed, or tranquil abiding meditation, and analytical or insight meditation. These are known as samatha and vipassana, respectively. Though they are quite different and can be practiced separately, meditators usually alternate between the two methods. The purpose of both practices is to gain some control over the mind. In this way we can say that meditation trains or transforms the mind.

Though insight meditation is generally considered more effective than calm meditation, there is not much point in trying to practice this analytical meditation until the mind is calm. Therefore we start with tranquil abiding meditation to help our mind become peaceful. Because tranquil abiding meditation is so effective in calming the mind, and facilitating single-pointed concentration, it is often practiced for 10 minutes or so before doing any of the other meditations described here. All are more effective if we bring our full attention to whatever we're practicing, whether sitting meditation or movement meditation.

Calm meditation can be practiced in the middle of another meditation session if the mind becomes excited and starts to race from thought to thought or if strong feelings arise and cause emotional turbulence. Once calm has been restored, then it is appropriate to simply continue with the analytical meditation, yoga, t'ai chi, or whatever meditation method was being used. On the other hand, if the mind becomes dull and heavy, or sleepy while practicing calm meditation, then analytical or movement meditation, even simple walking meditation, can restore clarity and alertness.

we start with tranquil abiding
meditation to help our mind
become peaceful

In meditation we withdraw from the external world and examine the inner world. Usually the mind looks outside itself, avidly latching on to external phenomena, and seems unconcerned with its own nature. We need to remember that our mind is in our body and tune into that rather than looking outside ourselves and latching onto superficial things around us. However, once we try to control our mind and ground it in our body, our sensory experiences become more noticeable and endlessly fascinating. This is because we have turned our attention inward instead of focusing on external phenomena, and our mind grasps at whatever it can – in this case our sensory experiences – rather than rests in its natural state. But focusing on these sensory experiences and sensations and being drawn into them is no more meditation than following our thoughts and fantasies.

transforming the mind

Although meditation is described as training and transforming the mind, this does not mean trying to control it by suppressing the thoughts and feelings that naturally arise. What we try to do is watch our thoughts, bodily sensations, and feelings as they arise, and recognize them as thoughts, sensations, and feelings rather than just being led along by them blindly. Some people find labeling these contents of the mind helpful and make inward comments such as, "This is a thought about what I might have for dinner tonight," or "This is a painful sensation in my leg." Such labeling can help you not indulge the thought or not be swept away by the feeling or sensation.

An analogy of the mind being like the deep ocean is often used when describing the nature of the mind. The ocean has hidden depths we are not immediately aware of because what we first encounter are the waves, which are like our thoughts and feelings. In the same way that waves rise out of the ocean and are swallowed up by its vast expanse, so thoughts arise in our mind and are effortlessly absorbed back into it. What we are aiming for in meditation is to gain a glimpse, or several, of the ocean itself, some elusive moments between the end of one thought and the beginning of another.

We can approach meditation in the same way we would cross a busy road. First we must stop, notice where we are, and focus on what we are going to do. This is like practicing calm meditation when we stop mindlessly following our thoughts and bring our attention firmly into the present. Then we look at the cars

as they go past and wait for a gap in the traffic, like watching our thoughts arise and pass, looking deeply at them using insight meditation. Finally, when there is an empty road, it is safe to cross. The empty road is like the nature of the mind, clear and with no obstructions, that leads us safely away from the rushing stream of thoughts. Though obviously our thoughts are not dangerous like passing traffic, they threaten our peace and calm in the same way that cars threaten our safety if we are not mindful when we cross the road.

We need to find a balance in which we are not suppressing thoughts and feelings but not indulging them either. In doing so we let the mind flow of its own accord and rest in its natural state. The mind does not have to think thoughts; it can simply be what it is. In practice, of course, this is much more difficult than it sounds. Since we have spent our whole lives thinking and fantasizing without questioning the process, it is difficult to change overnight. Meditation aims to change the way that we use our mind as well as our understanding of its true nature. Seeing the true nature of the mind, however, requires time and practice.

So is meditation even worth the effort at all? Yes, but we gain as much from the trying as from any notion of "success." Though we may not realize the nature of the mind in a few months, we will have developed a technique that allows us to find peace and calm, a quiet stillness beyond the hustle and bustle of daily life. We also learn a lot about our thought patterns and how our feelings change. Being aware, for example, that you have a tendency to think pessimistically about things gives you the opportunity to apply a remedy. When the usual pessimistic thoughts arise, you can remind yourself that this is just your thought pattern and actively try to think more positively. In this way meditation is a powerful tool that can improve the quality of your life.

as meditators we have the
opportunity to explore the depths
of our own mind

Scientists are endlessly curious about the nature of physical phenomena. They want to discover what lies in outer space and inside volcanoes. Mountaineers feel compelled to climb the highest mountains. As meditators we have the opportunity to explore the depths of our own mind, an equally fascinating journey that requires only the willingness to start practicing meditation and the determination to keep going. We can now embark on our own inner journey toward discovering inner calm, discovering the immeasurable benefits of meditation that have been acknowledged for centuries.

why meditate?

Many people start to meditate in order to find inner peace and calm. This is a good initial motivation to meditate, because we have made a conscious decision to alleviate the stress in our lives. Perhaps we have become disillusioned with our lifestyle; perhaps work, the gym, and social events have lost their ability to fulfill us. We want something different, to be able to step back from all these activities and discover what lies beyond this perpetual cycle of activity.

We might wonder why the material objects, activities, and relationships with people that were once so exciting and satisfying no longer hold the same appeal. Though these things bring happiness for a while, they do not have any lasting or intrinsic ability to make us truly happy. Why is this? Advertising, magazines, and contemporary media tell us that if we acquire all these possessions and relationships, then we will be happy. But we know from our own experience that often, once we've obtained the thing we have lusted after, we start wanting something else.

Everyone wants happiness, and we all have the right to try to find it in whatever way we choose so long as this does not involve hurting others or the environment. Understanding that new clothes, a vacation, the latest CD, or even a new relationship cannot bring lasting happiness is important. All things are impermanent; they arise and pass and therefore have no inherent ability to give us true happiness. How we relate to objects and people is also impermanent, which we realize once they stop making us happy. There is nothing wrong with any of these things or the temporary happiness they bring, but if we really want to find lasting happiness we must look elsewhere. Otherwise we will spend our lives chasing rainbows, looking for one temporary gratification after another and wasting the opportunity to find true contentment.

The decision to try to find happiness beyond external objects leads to a path of inner discovery. Our own mind contains the seeds of potential happiness, and meditation is the way to explore our mind and develop this potential into real happiness. I remember listening to a wise old Tibetan teacher many years ago at a public talk in London. He clearly saw how many of us there had failed to gain the happiness we hoped to achieve through a materialistic lifestyle. With great compassion and great humor, he told us how he had just listened to a song called "I Can't Get No Satisfaction" by a man called Rolling Stone. He thought that if Rolling Stone stopped rolling and sat and meditated for a while, he might find the satisfaction he obviously craved. The audience was in fits of laughter, but the message reached out and touched our hearts.

the benefits of meditation

The other benefits of meditation become obvious when we start to meditate regularly, and knowing about these might provide the inspiration to start. A major concern in our largely urban lifestyle is stress-related illness. The chances of suffering a heart attack or cancer have increased significantly as the pace of life becomes more frenetic. Our bodies were not designed to work and play this hard and can be pushed only so far before they respond with disease, their only way of telling us to slow down. Meditation is good for the body as well as the mind, helping prevent illness by dealing with stress before it becomes a serious problem.

The physical forms of meditation such as yoga and t'ai chi are particularly useful to calm and ground the body and help the meditator to be really present to how it feels. However, human beings are not composed of a separate body and mind; these are interdependent and the condition of one affects the other. When the body feels stressed, the mind is probably affected as well. Thus the issue of health is also relevant to our mind and emotions; meditation can bring wholeness and health to our entire person – body, mind, and emotions.

Suffering is an inescapable fact of life; there is no one who has not suffered. Some kinds of suffering are more subtle than others, and these can be better understood through meditation. In pictures of war, for example, the suffering is terrible and obvious. However, if we meditate that all things are impermanent – that everything wears out and turns to dust – we realize that everything is subject to change. Change is a lesser form of suffering. When our favorite objects break or are stolen, when we return from vacation and go back to work, we experience the suffering of change. Also, our bodies will grow old, get sick, and eventually die, and these changes bring suffering, too. We have a tendency to try to forget this.

Some meditation practices encourage us to contemplate the fact that one day we must die. Such practices are not morbid, simply realistic, because when we reflect on the reality and inevitability of our own death we realize how precious our life is and start to appreciate and enjoy it more. In this way meditation grounds us in the present moment so that we can say, "I am here now in this moment in time that keeps arising and passing and can feel the simple joy of being alive."

Reflecting upon the certainty of our death helps us gain perspective on other issues. Something that seemed so important, that has worried us and dominated our thoughts, can suddenly seem insignificant when we realize that one day we will die. Perhaps we have obsessed about an incident at work, when a colleague said or did something that was hurtful or upsetting. But in the larger context of life and death, is it really so important? Meditation can help us to see things in perspective, let go, and move on from incidents that are, in the grand scheme of things, quite trivial.

When we meditate we practice being here and now. We have the opportunity to check out who we really are, beyond the usual labels: "I am a mother, an architect, a musician." We realize we don't have to be anyone, we can just be. This brings immense relief, discovering there is nothing to live up to, and a kind of self-knowledge. Consequently we find it easier to accept ourselves just as we are without unhelpful comparisons to others and without putting ourselves down for not being good enough. In doing so, we can heal ourselves through meditation. Some people are led to meditation by existential concerns or wanting to discover the meaning of life. The British Buddhist author Stephen Batchelor says meditation and mystery are inseparable; when we meditate we open ourselves to the mystery of life itself. Inquiring into the mysterious nature of existence is a good

starting point for meditation, because one of the most useful things we can bring to our meditation practice is curiosity and a mind that keeps on questioning.

So there are many reasons why we meditate. You may have other personal reasons for meditating, and these are equally valid. It is helpful to understand why you want to meditate, but it is even more important to move on from thinking about meditation to actually practicing it. It is all too easy simply to read and think about meditation, perhaps talking about it with others, without ever getting around to actually meditating. Taking the first steps to meditation may initially be daunting, but once we've started we can begin to experience some of the many benefits mentioned here. Now let's consider what meditation actually is, in preparation for starting our meditation practice.

advice for beginners

The most important advice is to find a teacher, even if this is just a friend who has some experience meditating. The best way to start meditating, after reading about it and trying it out, is to join a meditation group. A meditation group is useful because a teacher or peers can help with many of the questions that will arise for you as a beginner. If you rely solely on your own experience, you may not know if you are doing it correctly or if your experience is normal or beneficial. Meditation is not an activity that brings instant gratification in the way of so many modern activities, so it is easy to become discouraged and feel like giving up. Here again, the support of friends who meditate is important. They can encourage you through the tough times and enjoy sharing your experiences when your meditation starts to flow. In time you too can be a support to other meditating friends. If you experience any mental disturbances at all during or after your meditation session, then ask your teacher for advice.

meditation can open our minds to new

levels of understanding about ourselves

and the world around us

Practicing meditation is an internal process of becoming familiar with the mind and helps us develop insight into ourselves, how we think and feel. So being completely open to our experiences when we meditate is important. We already have a personal world view of how we believe things exist and why people interact the way they do, but meditation can open our minds to new levels of understanding about ourselves and the world around us. Perhaps the world does not exist in exactly the way we think it does, and we can learn something new if we are prepared to modify our understanding of existence.

Sometimes the hardest thing we can do is start a new endeavor. With meditation, often the hardest thing to do is to continue practicing. It is easy to become discouraged in the beginning when our mind seems most resistant to what we want it to do. Instead of finding a state of spacious calm, our mind seems more chaotic than ever. But meditating frequently and regularly will give your mind time to calm down and experience all the benefits of meditation. Making a personal commitment to try it out for at least a month will help you. You'll soon find that starting and keeping your meditation practice going is not so difficult.

Once you have made a commitment to start meditating, you will need to find an appropriate time and place. Sticking to the same time and place helps meditation become a regular habit, something you do consistently rather than just occasionally. Privacy is important. Though the support of your meditating friends is beneficial, and you may meditate in a group sometimes, your personal meditation is something you do alone. Others may not understand why you want to meditate or may even think it's strange, perhaps fearing what they don't know. So choosing a time and place when it is easy to be private makes sense.

The best place for meditation is a room that only you use, but because this is not always possible, simply choose the best place available. Creative use of screens, other furniture, or large plants can make a corner of a room quite private. Choosing a place that is not affected by the noise of traffic, other people, or machinery is best.

Early morning, just after getting up, is a great time for meditation, since our mind is clear and not yet distracted by the activities of the day. It may seem a huge sacrifice to get out of bed a bit earlier when you begin your meditation practice, but in time the benefits will make it worthwhile.

It can be equally beneficial to make meditation the last activity of the day, just before going to bed. This creates an opportunity to reflect on the day's activities and let go of anything that disturbed the mind during the day. Meditation facilitates a good night's sleep by bringing the mind to a calm, peaceful state. However, if nothing particularly bothered you during the day, you have to be careful not to fall asleep during meditation. If this happens regularly, you probably need to change the time you meditate.

When you start, try out different times and places to find your optimum situation. Also experiment with the different positions – a cushion on the floor, meditation stool, or chair – to discover which one is most comfortable for you. When you have found a time, place, and meditation position that all work well for you, decide how often you want to meditate. Every day is best, but if this seems too ambitious at first try every working day, allowing two days off each week. Your meditation needs to be at least every other day to be effective, but whatever you decide, really try to stick to it.

practicing meditation little and often

When we first begin to meditate we need to start with short periods of time, so little and often is best. Ten or fifteen minutes is a good length of time for beginners to meditate, although this may seem quite long in the first few meditation sessions. If it seems too long, then shorten the meditation session to five or ten minutes. The length of time can always be increased, but if overdone at the start, it can be counterproductive.

It's useful to think of meditation like exercise. Most of us have had the experience of suddenly deciding we need to get fit or lose weight. We run off to the gym, do an hour of exercise, come home feeling virtuous, but end up with sore muscles the next day. Then we often give up because it is too painful to carry on. The next time we try to get fit, we start slowly and build up to longer periods of exercise. Just as this is more beneficial to our body, starting slowly and building up the length of time we meditate is more beneficial to our mind.

Meditation is not competitive. If you try to meditate for longer than is comfortable, you may become frustrated, bored, angry, or mentally tired. This may cause you to think meditation doesn't work, and you may decide to give it up in frustration. It is a sign of maturity and wisdom rather than weakness to start with ten minutes, increasing the time by five minutes when you feel ready.

The opposite reaction is also possible. Feeling lazy, you may decide to meditate for only five minutes instead of ten. Then, the next time you decide to meditate you may think it more fun to watch television instead. Before you know it, your meditation practice has disappeared before it ever really began. In our hectic lives meditation is a luxury, giving us personal time and mental and emotional space to simply be and to investigate how that feels. It is certainly worthwhile to create a 15-minute space every day to meditate. Everyone who wants to meditate can; it doesn't depend on money or being well educated. In meditation we are all equal.

common problems

Many of us may have a fantasy about the perfect meditation session, where the mind is calm and does not become distracted. We watch our thoughts arise and pass and don't get caught up in following them. We resist the temptation to fantasize about the future or indulge in nostalgic memories of the past. Our attention remains calmly on the in-breath and the out-breath. However, this idealized vision is rarely a reality. Accepting imperfection from the beginning is more fruitful than expecting perfect meditation experiences.

The most common problem when we start to meditate is thinking we can't do it. When we begin to watch our breathing and thoughts arising and passing, our mind often starts racing instead of experiencing peace and calm. We seem to be having far more thoughts than usual, and our mind seems incapable of not following them. Then, after being immersed in a particular thought or memory for some minutes, we guiltily realize that this is what we have been doing. We realize we haven't been watching our breath. Our thoughts arise and we just think them, so we begin to feel that meditation is beyond our grasp.

the most common problem

when we start to meditate

is thinking we can't do it

This is a common reaction at first, but over the course of several sessions the mind does eventually calm down. Because our mind has spent many years without supervision, just rambling through random fantasies and thoughts, it is easy to understand why it rebels when we begin to investigate how it works. This habitual mental wandering is the direct opposite of the focused concentration of meditation. Such habits are notoriously difficult to break, as we probably all know from experience, but not impossible if we have the motivation and commitment to make the change.

Patience is needed to allow the mind time to adjust to the changes brought about by meditation. Like a wild animal that needs taming, it takes time and effort to transform the mind's unrestrained mental wandering and exert some measure of control over it. Just as you would be kind and patient to an animal that needs taming, be kind to yourself and give meditation a chance to calm your mind.

The opposite problem of an overactive mind, sleepiness or mental lethargy, can also happen, though usually only after a few meditation sessions when the initial excitement has worn off. This is the mind and body responding to another of our usual habits: that when we become still and quiet we are often preparing for sleep. Mental dullness can also arise from laziness or not trying hard enough. Though meditation is concerned with creating mental calmness, it is not an idle state and takes considerable effort.

the need for constant vigilance

Above all, meditation requires constant vigilance of what state the mind is in. When we notice our mind has become sleepy, we need to stimulate ourselves into alertness. Remind yourself of the benefits of meditation and then return to your meditation practice. If that doesn't work, you may have been meditating for too long and need a break. If you still wish to carry on meditating or have only just started, practice walking meditation to alleviate drowsiness. Walking meditation in nature and the fresh air is gently stimulating if the weather conditions are not distracting; however, walking meditation in a howling gale is not conducive to focused concentration!

In addition to mental excitement and dullness, there is also the possibility of physical discomfort and pain to contend with during a meditation session. Practicing one of the physically active meditation techniques, such as yoga or t'ai chi, is a good way to relax the body. These dynamic meditations work on both mental and physical levels to alleviate tension and make the mind and body comfortable. They both work with the energies flowing through our body, which improves our bodily awareness, bringing our attention inside ourselves and noticing how the body feels. So when we start a sitting meditation the body is more receptive to sitting quietly and relaxed, but not in a soporific state.

developing awareness of the body

Another technique can be practiced during the sitting meditation itself. This is mentally sweeping through the entire body, paying attention to all the different parts. It is best to start at the top of the body with the head and work downward. First we bring awareness to the body part we want to begin work with (the head, for example). Simply observe how this part of your body feels. Is there stress and tension? Does it feel tight, cramped, or painful? Is it overly relaxed and slumped over? Stay with the observation for a minute or so, just letting your concentration dwell there.

If there is stress or discomfort of some kind, then try to relax this consciously by breathing into the area. Although this may sound a little strange if you've never done it before, simply take a deep breath in and visualize the breath as it travels

around your body to the part you want as you breathe out. Or you can imagine the discomfort dissolving or evaporating with the exhalation. If the discomfort persists, then keep your attention in this area, and just mentally observe what is going on. Sometimes these aches and pains go away by themselves. Not moving immediately when we feel discomfort allows the body the opportunity to adjust itself.

If the discomfort intensifies or is overwhelming, then simply change your position to alleviate the pain. Meditation is a mental activity to promote calm and not an endurance test to see how much pain can be tolerated. If you do need to move, keep this simple and short so as not to interfere with the meditation.

Sometimes there is the temptation to fidget, but try to resist it. This is the mind wanting something to distract it from the meditative inquiry. In the same way the mind resists sitting still and concentrating, the body responds by wanting to fidget, so move only when it is necessary to alleviate discomfort.

Meditation is powerful and we may notice unusual images arising in the mind. Our body may feel heavy or light or like it has shrunk or expanded in some way. A very few people might experience the feeling of the mind floating outside the body, usually only a short distance above. Such experiences are quite normal, though unusual, and are not harmful in any way, so there is no need to worry. Reactions like these simply indicate that the mind is becoming accustomed to a new activity, focusing inward on itself. Experiences of this kind do not indicate any great advances in meditation either. They are neither good nor bad, just unusual sensations that happened to occur. We should not try to encourage or resist these experiences, feeling neither attraction nor aversion. The key to meditation is simply observing what happens in our mind and feelings without making any kind of judgment.

when painful feelings and memories arise

Some painful feelings and memories, which have been repressed or forgotten, will inevitably come to mind.

Try to treat these in the same way as pleasant recollections by simply letting them go. In the unlikely event you experience something that bothers you deeply or makes you feel uncomfortable, simply stop the meditation.

Try to find a meditation teacher who can talk with you about your experience and provide advice. Feeling a bit disheartened at times is normal when we begin to meditate.

Because we have not previously paid this amount of dispassionate attention to our inner life, we notice things that may not have been apparent to us before. Although meditation does not cause our mental experiences, it does help us to become aware of them. All the distractions and random pursuit of thoughts were always there; we just never noticed them before. So have courage and be patient as you embark on the path of meditation.

sitting meditations

correct posture

Correct posture is an important aspect of all meditation techniques. With movement meditations such as yoga, posture is more important and complex than sitting positions, because if a movement is performed incorrectly, there is the possibility of pulling muscles or other body injury. Even with sitting meditations, the correct posture can help minimize physical discomfort. However, correct posture is fundamentally important to allow the energy of the body to move freely.

This is one reason why finding a teacher is always recommended when beginning any new meditation discipline. Joining a group not only gives access to instructions and advice from a teacher but also provides a peer group for friendship and support. However, with the various meditation techniques described here, there are sufficient instructions given to allow safe experimentation. If any of the simple guided exercises in this book particularly appeal to you, then the resource list at the back can help you find teachers and groups for further study and practice.

the importance of a straight back

The most important aspect of meditation postures is a straight back. When the spine is aligned in a straight line, our energies flow freely throughout our body, facilitating a meditative state. Many of the body's energies flow through our nervous system, of which the spinal cord is the basis; thus keeping a straight back allows our energies to flow freely along the spine. The mind and body rely on each other, and a straight back is more comfortable when sitting still for a while, even though it may take time to become accustomed to such a posture. There are plenty of mental and emotional distractions without the added discomfort caused by bad posture during meditation.

The classic posture used by meditators over the centuries is sitting cross-legged on a meditation cushion (called a *zafu*) on the floor. However, this is not always comfortable and is certainly not essential. Many people prefer to use a meditation stool, which allows you to sit with a straight back and the legs tucked underneath the stool. Even more simple, you can sit in a chair with both feet resting flat on the floor. It is important to sit upright and not lean back to support the back, because doing so means the back will no longer be straight. However, if you have genuine back problems, this may be more comfortable, though always try to sit with a straight back if you can. We can remember the Zen saying "Sit straight and be straight in the practice."

posture

If you start meditating in the correct posture from the beginning, your meditation will benefit. It is difficult to rest in stillness because although the body is motionless the mind runs riot with thoughts. However, the body's stillness will eventually help the mind become calm.

correct posture for sitting meditations

These basic instructions apply whether you are sitting on a meditation cushion, meditation stool, or chair.

I   Sit in a relaxed manner, not too stiff and not so relaxed that your body is slumped, remembering to keep your back straight. Position your head so it is inclined slightly forward. Keep your eyes partly open and looking down at a gentle angle. This helps prevent sleepiness, but if your eyes wander to objects and your attention becomes distracted, then keep your eyes loosely shut.

2   Keep your hands gently folded and resting in your lap, with the palms facing upward and one hand on top of the other. An alternative is to rest one hand on each knee, either face up or down, whichever is more comfortable.

3   Aim for a relaxed posture, free from tension. In this way, the body supports the mind and helps it to be clear and calm. Some discomfort will inevitably arise from sitting still, but try to find a balance between fidgeting and experiencing unpleasant body sensations. A good way to know if you really need to move is to simply observe each sensation of discomfort as it arises and not react immediately. If the discomfort continues or becomes worse, then you should quietly adjust your position, but sometimes the sensation will pass naturally.

calm meditation

Now that we have prepared ourselves and found a suitable time and place, we can begin an actual meditation session. Calm, or tranquil abiding, meditation is based on mindfulness of breathing, which means we watch our breaths, being mindful of each inhalation and each exhalation as they happen in time. Through calm meditation we can start to understand the nature of the mind beyond discursive thought as well as why our lives often seem permeated with dissatisfaction and suffering.

through calm meditation we can start to understand the nature of the mind beyond discursive thought as well as why our lives often seem permeated with dissatisfaction

When we are inclined to turn away from worldly concerns we are ready to practice sitting meditation. We might be inspired by some spiritual impulse such as wishing to feel closer to God, to experience *atman* – the transcendental or universal Self beyond the "I," ego, or personal sense of self – or realize our innate Buddhanature – the potential within us all to attain enlightenment and become a buddha. But it is the desire for inner peace, an existential response to the human condition, that for many people provides the initial impulse to practice meditation.

focusing on the breath

Calm meditation focuses our attention on the breath, so we become aware of the moment-to-moment process of breathing. We do not attempt to change the breathing in any way or indeed do anything to interfere with our experience, so we don't judge our breathing as "good" or "bad," "shallow" or "deep." This puts us in touch with our whole physical continuum, our body together with all the various mental, emotional, and physical sensations we experience. After some time this makes us feel calm and centered, and – if we are fortunate – we might experience a profound and deep inner peace.

Once we have attained some inner calm, we extend mindfulness of breathing into mindful awareness of our body, feelings, mind, and thoughts, which are sometimes called the four foundations of mindfulness. We watch our thoughts

sitting meditations

32

arise and pass and try not to follow or indulge them, seeking to experience the nature of the mind before thoughts arise. We simply become aware of a thought, label it "a thought," and let it go.

However, these simple instructions are not so easy to follow. The mind may rebel at being asked to change its usual habit of indulging memories, fantasies, and thoughts. It is common for beginners to feel that their mind is out of control, that they cannot meditate at all. Yet this is meditation, just the willingness to sit down and try, being aware of the turbulence of the mind, and not judging the process as "not being able to meditate."

who am I?

When we become aware of the fact that we are not the master of our mind, if we accept it and simply keep bringing our attention back to our breathing, paradoxically we do experience calm and peace after some time. Gradually we accept that our mind is not under our control as we had at first assumed, and we realize meditation is a discipline that helps us to be aware of the mind and the natural process of thoughts arising and passing. Attempts to control this process, rather than simply being aware of it, are doomed to failure because the nature of the mind is beyond any concept of control. After watching our thoughts for some time, the question "Who am I?" no longer has the same simple answer we used to think, because our sense of self changes from moment to moment. These are the first steps toward the liberating freedom that meditation can help us to discover.

With diligence and perseverance in the practice of mindfulness of breathing and mindful awareness, gradually the mind quiets and concentration improves. The temptation to follow thoughts and indulge fantasies and memories is easier to resist. The initial mental turbulence settles into a calm stillness. This restful inner peace reduces stress and tension and is a real refuge from the frenetic activity of daily life.

gradually we accept that our mind

is not under our control as we

had at first assumed

We might wonder why something as simple as calm meditation has such a powerful effect, but if we consider the nature of breathing this becomes clear. We need to breathe regularly and continuously from our first inhalation at birth to our last exhalation at death. If we do not breathe for more than a few minutes we die. Yet how often are we aware of this precious life-sustaining action of breathing? We tend to take breathing for granted because our body does it unconsciously, but this is why we are able to sleep and breathe at the same time.

There is a variety of techniques to help you stay aware of watching your breath when you begin to meditate. If you have a logical disposition and like numbers, then you can try mentally counting the breaths. For each complete breath, in and out, make a mental note of one, two, and so on. When you notice a thought arise, return to one and start again. On the other hand, if you have a strong visual sense, you might like to imagine the sea moving with the tide. With each breath in, the sea withdraws and with each breath out, the waves move forward and break on the beach. Be careful to watch the breaths and not get lost in the ocean. If you usually think in words, you might prefer to think "love" as you breathe in and "peace" as you breathe out. Be careful to use the words only to help you watch the breath. You can choose any or none of these techniques to help; they are simply options if they appeal to you.

we simply realize that we are a

part of the world around us, not

the center of the universe

When we meditate we gradually become aware of the preciousness of being alive. The mundane matters with which we were so preoccupied before slowly recede and fade away. We realize that we are here and now, alive in this moment, and that this is our most important concern. As we breathe air in and out, we notice our interaction with the immediate surroundings outside ourselves and how we depend on our environment to sustain us.

This can be a humbling experience because we normally feel we are in control of our lives, but it also allows us to accept ourselves as we are, with all our imperfections. There is no judgment in simply being aware of our interdependence with our surroundings. We simply realize that we are a part of the world around us, not the center of the universe. This calm self-acceptance can be a healing experience, helping us let go of our neurotic obsessions, our self-criticism, fears, and doubts.

preparing for calm meditation

There are two ways of preparing for meditation, outer and inner. We have already looked at the outer preparations in choosing a conducive time and place. Inner preparation is checking how you feel and ensuring you are not too tired or too excited to meditate.

instructions for calm meditation

1   Settle quietly into the meditation posture, either on a meditation cushion, meditation stool, or on a chair. Set an alarm clock for 10 minutes, and then forget about the time. Make sure your whole body is relaxed and comfortable and your back is straight.

2   Make the commitment to try to meditate as well as you can and to let go of your thoughts, fantasies, and memories.

3   Bring your attention to your breathing by becoming aware of the sensation at the tip of the nostrils as breath enters and leaves your body. If you prefer, you can focus on the sensation of your abdomen rising and falling with each inhalation and exhalation.

4   Be mindful to watch the breath without judging the process; you are being aware of your breathing but are not trying to change it in any way. Remember that you are in the present moment, here and now, and that all you have to do is be mindful of your breathing.

5   When a thought arises, be aware of it as just a thought and watch it dissipate. You do not have to follow it, however attractive that might seem. You have made the decision to meditate for 10 minutes, and you can think all your thoughts afterward.

6   Your mind may wander a lot at first, so don't be too hard on yourself when you notice that you have been following a thought or indulging a memory or fantasy. Gently bring your attention back to the breath, and try to keep it there.

7   When the alarm rings, open your eyes and shift your position, but do not immediately rush off to do something. Take a minute or two to evaluate the experience. If it seemed too long, then shorten your next meditation session to five or seven minutes. If it seemed like no time at all, then increase the time to 15 minutes. Resolve to meditate again soon. Then move thoughtfully into your daily life.

insight meditation

Calm meditation brings tranquillity and peace and is the foundation for all sitting meditations as we learned in Chapter One. However, from a spiritual perspective this peace is not an end in itself, pleasant though it may be. It is a stage in training the mind to develop an understanding of our habits, behavior, and motivations. It will help us learn how to distinguish between actions that lead to suffering or dissatisfaction and actions that bring happiness. As meditative awareness progresses, it leads to an understanding that craving, attachment, delusion, and ignorance of how things truly exist are the root of human suffering.

This insight is the combined aim of mindful awareness and analysis of thoughts and feelings – to develop an understanding of what causes unhappiness and therefore avoid the mental and physical actions that cause it. After all, it is one of the fundamental truths of existence that everyone wants happiness and to avoid suffering. The problem is that we usually mistake temporary gratification for happiness and stay trapped in a cycle that repeatedly leads to dissatisfaction.

Insight meditation therefore unites the calm mind, developed from mindfulness of breathing during calm meditation, with insightful understanding that comes from analyzing our thoughts and feelings. This analysis is sometimes called penetrative seeing or insight, derived from the Pali (the ancient Indian language in which the Buddha's words were first written) word for penetrative seeing, vipassana. Insight meditation eventually leads to an understanding that liberates us from both attachment and delusion and brings us to a state of authentic happiness.

This powerful sitting meditation has been practiced extensively by many contemplatives, particularly from the Eastern traditions of Buddhism and Hinduism. However, variations exist in all the religions. Wisdom is universal and available to anyone, whatever their belief system. In Christianity the contemplative or mystic describes his or her insights as being given by God, whereas the Sufi believes he or she is not separate from God and that insights arise from realizing this oneness with God. In another way, the Buddhist meditator believes insights come from his or her own innate Buddhanature.

However, the wisdom and understanding derived through insight meditation transcend all belief systems, even those of people who have no religion. In this way, both calm meditation and insight meditation can be practiced by anyone, even together with people of different belief systems. It unites people beyond the different languages and forms of the various religions, focusing on what we have in common – our human nature – rather than any superficial distinctions. However, usually someone who wants to meditate seriously has well-developed spiritual values, whether these are traditional or personal.

sitting meditations

So meditation is useful for all people, whether an individual is religious or not. Meditation is, in essence, simply training the mind. Once the mind has developed some single-pointed concentration through calm meditation, we move onto insight meditation, which is ultimately more effective because of our intelligence and the power of our discriminating awareness. This means we keep questioning, keep inquiring, and try to find logical reasons for the contents of our thoughts and feelings and why they arise and pass in the way they do.

Once we gain some understanding about the contents of our mind and how thoughts arise and pass, we can take our inquiry further. The question arises of what we will do with this newfound self-knowledge, what is its purpose? Self-knowledge derived through insight meditation can help us learn to solve our problems by developing wisdom. Within the different religious traditions wisdom is described as purifying delusions, giving light and strength, or mirrorlike wisdom clearly reflecting our mind. The wisdom that arises through insight meditation is accompanied by the spirit of love and compassion, because wisdom is inseparable from ethics. But the prime purpose of wisdom at this stage is to shine light on our thoughts and feelings.

letting go

Once the mind has become quiet through calm meditation, we start to look at our thoughts and feelings, really probing deeply and analyzing what we find. This is quite a radical process, openly confronting the contents of our mind, and sometimes causes old repressed and painful memories to surface. This can be disturbing at first and seems to increase suffering by remembering these half-forgotten past traumatic events. However, if we never dealt with these painful situations at the time, we can analyze the memory of them now, letting them go and lessening their hold over our mind and emotions.

Once a painful memory arises, we allow this to rest in our consciousness, simply letting it be. We do not judge the memory and the subsequent feeling nor do we allow ourselves to become afraid. Through analysis of the memory and feeling we can see their insubstantial nature and can remind ourselves that just as the old forgotten memory popped into our mind, it will leave again.

We do not have to identify with our past feelings, and we are not the same person as when we experienced the painful episode. Over time we have changed in many ways, both subtle and obvious, and analysis will tell us that we cannot be exactly the same person, although obviously we are connected with these past experiences. This puts the episode firmly in the past, so that when we look at the memory, it no longer has the same intensity or hold over us. In this way our greatest fears and deepest pains can gradually lessen over time with the repeated practice of insight meditation.

Of course sometimes insight meditation isn't as simple or straightforward as this. Old repressed memories can be deeply disturbing and all-consuming for as long as they last. When this happens, the best remedy is to return to calm meditation and simply watch the breath until the pain lessens and some concentration returns. Then we carry on with insight meditation. If the painful memory lingers, we stay with it, allowing it to rest in consciousness until it eventually dissipates. If other thoughts, feelings, and memories have arisen in the meantime, we simply work with whatever is there.

practicing insight meditation

In this meditation we will be moving between calm meditation and analytical meditation. Take as long as you like with the initial calm meditation. Without the single-pointed concentration developed through calm meditation, the insight meditation will not be so effective or powerful.

instructions for insight meditation

1   Begin with some minutes of calm meditation, watching the breaths come and go. Gradually the mind slows down, and you can start to observe your thoughts and feelings as they arise and pass.

2   Analyze your thoughts and feelings. This is not a superficial exercise and requires concentration on what has arisen in the mind. If your mind begins to wander, return to watching the breath until concentration becomes more focused and stable. If your mind continues to wander, gently return your concentration to your original subject.

3   Try hard to penetrate the thought or feeling with your intellect and question what you habitually think you know about it. Gradually you discover there are other ways to know about this thought as you allow your intuitive feelings to surface. You can think of insight meditation as an internal lecture or debate that questions all assumptions and looks at all possible lines of inquiry into thoughts and feelings.

4   Doubts, difficulties, and questions will continue to arise during your meditation, sometimes like a plague of insects, but stay with the process. Look at the doubts and questions carefully because you can learn from them. If the mind becomes deeply distracted, return to calm meditation for a few minutes.

5   Don't do too much insight meditation at first or the mind will become tired and perhaps want to reject the meditation process. In the beginning, between 10 and 20 minutes is long enough to experience the benefits of insight meditation. Gradually you can increase the length of the meditation session, after you have gained some experience.

letting go

visualization

Visualization, using our imagination to create mental images, is something we are all familiar with. When we go to sleep and dream, our unconscious mind creates vivid and often surreal sequences of images. When awake, sometimes we fantasize about the future, visualizing ourselves in an idealized chosen scenario. We spend time remembering the past and these memories are often visual, too. We also have daydreams and fall into reveries in which the mind wanders freely, and visual images and pictures effortlessly and spontaneously arise in the mind.

With such a proliferation of mental images to draw on, we obviously have a great capacity for visualization.

However, unless our work or hobby involves art, film, or another visual medium, we rarely develop this natural capacity for visualization. We usually take it for granted and are unaware of the process while it is happening. We just lose ourselves in the images, wandering aimlessly through our fantasies and memories, unconcerned about what we are doing. This is similar to mindlessly following our thoughts and feelings before we train our mind through meditation. Just as we learn in meditation to observe how our thoughts arise and pass, becoming aware that they are thoughts and resisting the desire to follow them, we can train our mind with various visualization meditation techniques.

Some visualization meditations have overtly religious and devotional associations, whereas others are designed to promote health and healing, and have no specific religious overtones. There are both simple and complex visualization methods. With some visualization meditations we mentally re-create physical objects, and with others we use pure imagination. Certain visualization meditations work with the analytical process of insight meditation, and others work with naturally occurring energy centers in the body (which we will explore in more detail later) and with breathing techniques. With such a range to choose from, it is best to look at a few basic principles first.

basic principles for using visualization in meditation

As with all sitting meditations, we start by sitting in one of the classic meditation postures, relaxed and comfortable before we begin. We watch our breath in calm meditation for a few minutes to quiet and clear our mind before beginning this more challenging form of meditation. We can use a physical object or abstract image; one is not better or more advanced than the other. However, it is important to choose a precise object or image. Otherwise the mind will flit from one object to another.

With visualization meditation, imagination is our most important asset and can become more vivid and creative if we practice regularly and often. We use our imagination to replicate a physical object or create a mental object in our mind. It is important to choose a suitable image or symbol. Some symbols have an inherent quality that helps us find a connection with our spiritual self, with humanity, with God, or with our own Buddhanature, or a sense of belonging to the world, being part of a whole. Such symbols are often referred to as archetypes and have inspired people for centuries to find spiritual meaning and inner peace. The objects and symbols that hold these archetypal qualities are appropriate for visualization meditation.

suitable objects of meditation

There is a beautiful story of a Buddhist abbot who felt inspired to meditate on the foremost symbol of Christianity, the cross. Though this symbol did not belong to his own religious and cultural tradition, he realized its significance to another major world religion. Retaining an open mind, he entered a deep visualization meditation on the Christian cross. During his meditation he gained the profound insight that the cross could also symbolize the cutting of the "I," a Buddhist method of relinquishing the power of the ego. In this way he came to a deeper appreciation of Christianity while refining his understanding of Buddhism. This story demonstrates clearly that symbols from one culture can provide powerful visualization objects for another, and that we have much to learn from each other's religions and cultures.

There are many suitable objects for visualization. As we saw from the story of the Buddhist abbot and the cross, religious symbols are useful. These include the Star of David, the yin yang circle, pictures of Mohammed, Jesus, Buddha, the Virgin Mary, Shiva, and the many other icons and deities of the world's religions. Some symbols are not overtly religious but carry associations of spiritual unity, such as the circle. Nature symbols are also suitable, reminding us of our connection with the earth, and we can use objects such as trees, flowers, lakes, and even the earth as seen from outer space. Visualization meditation with white or gold light can be healing.

If a physical object is to be used, place it in front of the meditation seat where it is easily visible. Look at the object with focused concentration. Notice even little details, as well as size, shape, and color. Then close your eyes and try to build up the object in your mind. Spend some time doing this without referring to the actual object. It is the visualization meditation that is important rather than total accuracy. If you experience problems, try visualizing a small part of the object rather than the whole thing and build up the mental image slowly.

It is useful to refer once or twice, depending on the length of the session, to the physical object during your visualization. This checks the overall progress of the visualization and is an opportunity to ensure that small details are accurate.

If an abstract object (one that is not present in front of you) is to be used, if possible first bring a specific image to mind. For example, rather than thinking of a general tree, think of the familiar oak tree in your park. Then, in the same way as with a physical object, attempt to build the image in your mind, remembering the little details as well as the more obvious features. If the visualization meditation becomes too frustrating, draw a blank screen across your mind and watch the breath in calm meditation for some minutes. When you return to your visualization object, you can try to build it up in a different way.

meditation on candlelight

This simple and joyful visualization meditation is a good one to start with. Spend about 15 minutes in the meditation or longer if you wish. You can keep the visualization simple the first time you do it and build up to a more complicated vision during subsequent sessions.

instructions for visualization meditation on candlelight

I   Sit comfortably in the meditation posture and practice a few minutes of calm meditation, watching the breath.

2   Visualize a tall, gleaming wax candle burning brightly. Notice the blue inner flame and the golden outer flame, the melted wax dripping down the sides, the blackness of the wick.

3   Visualize the bright light streaming into your heart, becoming brighter and filling your whole body with brilliant light. Visualize your whole body from the outside, brightly aglow and luminous like crystal.

4   Now imagine you are seated in a beautiful large room, a temple or place of worship if you like. You are surrounded by other people and the light from the candle streams toward each person in turn, filling them with light.

The light fills the room. Everything becomes radiant and translucent.

The light glows more vibrantly and flows out of the room, through the doors and windows. There is a tidal wave of light filling every person and object it touches, and the light keeps expanding until the town, country, and whole world is filled with light.

5   Return your attention to your own body, but keep the idea of the world full of light. The light is cleansing and healing. It fills you with the simple joy of being alive here and now.

energy centers
and channels

If we visualize our physical body and explore the various sensations inside it, we are often aware of the presence of subtle flowing energies. There is no physical proof for these and they won't be found in anatomy books. However, for centuries meditators, acupuncturists, and t'ai chi and yoga practitioners have been aware of their existence through direct practical experience of working with these energy centers and channels. In our Western, scientific, and rational way of thinking, we may find this idea a little strange. How can these things exist without some physical indications? But if we think of the Christian concept of the soul, this too cannot be found physically, yet its existence is generally accepted.

All these nonphysical energies are connected with religious practices, and working with them in the various disciplines can bring about higher levels of consciousness and enlightenment. Each discipline has its own specific methodology of how it interprets and works with these energy centers and channels. The acupuncturist, for example, inserts needles at specific points along certain channels, called meridians, to stimulate the flow of chi, or subtle energy, for the purposes of healing. Yoga and t'ai chi practitioners use movement and postures combined with breathing exercises to become aware of these energies and use them in physical meditation.

single-pointed concentration, visualization,

and breathing are combined in powerful

meditation practices

Probably the most profound use of energy centers and channels is found in the Hindu and Buddhist meditations, where single-pointed concentration, visualization, and breathing are combined in powerful meditation practices. It is important to remember that working with these energy centers and channels is complex and profound and differs slightly between the various systems, so we can make only a brief foray into this world of subtle energy. The Hindu Kundalini system is explained in the next chapter, so we will look at the Tibetan Buddhist system here.

In the Buddhist system, there are three main channels in the body, called *nadi* in Sanskrit, which comes from the root word *nad* meaning motion. These channels run up and down the body's torso, situated inside, slightly forward of the spine. Several energy centers, called channel wheels or *nadi*-chakras, intersect the three channels at key places. The main, central channel is pale blue on the outside and red inside. It is called the mind channel or Avadhuti (also sometimes called Sushumna like in the Hindu system) and runs from the tip of the sex organ in a straight line to the top of the head, where it then arches over and ends between the two eyebrows. On both sides of the central channel, but with no space between it and them, lie the right, red, solar channel called Rasana, and the left, white, lunar channel called Lalana.

Below the navel, the left channel curves slightly to the right, separating a little from the central channel and rejoining it at the tip of the sex organ. The right channel curves slightly to the left and ends at the tip of the anus. At four places the right and left channels coil around the central channel, forming knots known as chakras. These occur at the navel, the heart, the throat, and the crown of the head, forming four of the five main chakras, the remaining base chakra being at the sexual center or "secret place." Each chakra has spokes that branch out toward other parts of the body.

the most important is the first root wind,

called the life-supporting wind and situated at

the heart chakra, which functions to

support and maintain life

The crown chakra is called the Wheel of Great Bliss. It is white and triangular, and has 32 spokes arching downward. The throat chakra is called the Wheel of Enjoyment. It is red and circular and has 16 spokes arching upward. The heart chakra is called the Wheel of Phenomena. It is white and circular and has eight spokes arching downward. The navel chakra is called the Wheel of Emanation. It is red and triangular and has 64 spokes arching upward. The heart chakra is considered most important and is often described in considerably more detail.

During the meditations on these channels and chakras, we use our ordinary breath and subtle energy winds called prana. Like the nonphysical energetic nature of the channels and chakras, these winds are physically undetectable. They are called the moving winds because they flow through the channels and there are five root and five branch winds. The most important is the first root wind called the life-supporting wind and situated at the heart chakra, which functions to support and maintain life.

The main aim of using this system of meditation is to bring the winds into the central channel to help generate great bliss and enhance meditative concentration. In daily life the winds flow in the right and left channels, concentration is scattered, and conceptual thoughts arise, breaking single-pointed concentration. When the winds move within the central channel, thoughts do not arise to interrupt concentration, so meditation is powerful and penetrating.

Along with the channels, chakras, and winds are two types of drops, like tiny drops of liquid, red and white, gross and subtle. They are called *bindus*. The subtle red and white drops reside in the central channel in the heart chakra. During meditation, the gross red and white drops flow through the other channels, causing bliss, though the white drop resides mainly at the crown of the head and the red drop at the navel.

the ultimate aim of practicing meditation

within this system is to attain

enlightenment or nirvana

This is a simple explanation of a profound spiritual system, which is practiced by initiates under the guidance of a teacher or guru. The ultimate aim of practicing meditation within this system is to attain enlightenment or nirvana – the cessation of suffering and liberation from the endless cycle of birth, death, and rebirth. If this Tibetan Buddhist system appeals to you, then it is essential to find a teacher to explain things clearly. It can be dangerous to play around with these subtle energies if you are not experienced. However, with proper instruction and guidance this sophisticated meditation practice is ultimately very rewarding.

There are some simple preliminary meditations using these energy centers and channels that are both safe and beneficial to practice. We can use the three channels and five chakras in visualization meditation and in this way become familiar with them. We may even become aware of subtle energy, or prana, when we bring our attention to these areas.

the nine exhalations purification

This preliminary meditation is also known as dispelling the impure winds. The practice brings together breathing and visualization techniques in a powerful synergy that helps develop awareness of the three channels and the five chakras. If you have practiced some of the breathing and visualization meditations described earlier, this meditation, which unites the two methods, will not be difficult.

instructions for nine exhalations purification

1 As usual, start by relaxing into the meditation posture and spending a few minutes watching the breath in calm meditation. Make a fist with the right hand, using the four fingers to enclose the thumb. Then extend the index finger and use the back of it to block the left nostril.

2 Inhale a full deep breath through the right nostril. As you inhale, visualize the inspiring strength of all the Buddhas from all the different times and realms as radiant white light that flows from the right nostril down to the heart chakra and dissolves. Maintain the inhalation for as long as possible. Before exhaling, move your index finger to the right nostril to block it, using the front of the finger. When you exhale, make three equal breaths out with a slight pause between each. As you exhale, visualize that all the impure winds, especially those on the left-hand side of the body, are dispelled as black smoke.

3 Keeping your finger against the right nostril, inhale deeply through the left, visualizing the inspiring strength of the Buddhas as radiant white light. Hold this breath as long as possible, then exhale the impure winds visualized as black smoke, especially those on the right-hand side of the body, in three equal out-breaths through the left nostril, having closed the right nostril with the index finger.

4 Now rest your hands in your lap, palms upward, right hand on top of the left with the tips of the thumbs touching. Breathe in through both nostrils deeply while visualizing white light as before. Exhale in three equal out-breaths through both nostrils, visualizing black smoke as before. Reflect on the fact that all the channels, winds, and drops are now purified, supple, and comfortable.

5 Finish with calm meditation, watching the breath, retaining the feeling of purification.

other forms of meditation

walking
meditation

For centuries walking meditation, or contemplative walking, has been practiced both formally and informally in the various spiritual traditions. There is also pilgrimage, which in the past (before modern means of transport) meant walking to a holy place significant to one's religious tradition. In times past, in most religions people were supposed to make at least one pilgrimage during their lifetime. There is the sacred pilgrimage to Mecca for Muslims, for example, and even today most Muslims try to reach Mecca at least once in their lives. We may remember from our school days Chaucer's *Canterbury Tales*, which are life stories, often bawdy and entertaining rather than overtly religious, told by each pilgrim in turn to pass the time on the long Christian pilgrimage to Canterbury Cathedral.

in times past, in most religions
people were supposed to make
at least one pilgrimage during
their lifetime

circumambulation

Another form of holy contemplative walking is circumambulation of a sacred temple, a reliquary containing holy objects (called a *stupa* in Buddhism), or a holy mountain. Circumambulation is the circling of the sacred object by walking in a clockwise direction as a mark of devotion and respect and to "earn" merit. The famous Mount Kailash in Tibet is holy to both Buddhists and Hindus. This arduous circumambulation takes several days as well as the lengthy pilgrimage to get there. During pilgrimage and circumambulation, people pray, reflecting upon the meaning of their life and why they are undertaking the religious journey, a kind of informal walking meditation. However, we will focus on formal walking meditation here.

Because we practice mindful awareness and sometimes insight meditation during walking meditation, we can think of walking meditation as a different meditation posture rather than a whole new discipline. This is particularly relevant if we intend to spend a long time meditating. If, for example, we wish to spend a whole day in meditation, we can alternate between sessions of sitting and walking, of perhaps 30 minutes sitting and 10 minutes walking. Alternating between the two allows us to stretch cramped muscles and ease the pain and stiffness that accumulate through sitting.

korean zen

In Korean Zen meditation practice, the formal sessions are split into 50 minutes sitting, followed by 10 minutes walking. Meditation is practiced inside a large meditation hall with the cushions arranged systematically around the center with space behind them for walking. This style of walking meditation is brisk, more like a march than a walk, and really exercises the muscles and joints. The benefit of this is apparent when we learn that in Korean monasteries the monks and nuns usually meditate like this between 10 and 14 hours a day for three months at a time. However, this style of walking meditation is unique to the Korean Zen tradition.

walking for the sake of walking

The more usual method of walking meditation is performed at a contemplative and unusually slow pace. The whole point of the walking meditation is the walking; there is no concern with any destination or reflection about where we have come from. To facilitate this, many people undertake walking meditation in a clearly defined short line of between 10 and 20 meters, and then simply turn around and retrace their steps. Sometimes there is a short pause after turning around and before resuming the walking, to assist mindful awareness of the practice.

When we practice walking meditation, the experience is quite distinct from sitting meditation because the body is moving. The experience is also different from walking in order to get somewhere.

Usually we take walking for granted. We don't even think about what we are doing when we are doing it, and we remain largely unconcerned with how we are doing it. Our concern is about where we are going and what we will do when we get there. Otherwise we are lost in our usual thoughts and fantasies. In this way, walking meditation is quite radical. All those preoccupations and distractions are put to one side or taken away, leaving us with the bare experience of walking.

Because the bare experience of walking is the meditation, we can take the moving body as our meditation object or our focus of awareness.

Because we are doing it so slowly, we have plenty of time to really feel the subtlety of each movement and try to be completely present to the whole experience. The internationally acclaimed Vietnamese Buddhist teacher Thich Nhat Hanh describes walking meditation in this way: "One walks in file, very slowly, silently with the eyes lowered. Mindfulness is maintained while walking, taking one step with the left foot while breathing in and one step with the right foot while breathing out." We can also practice walking meditation in this way, coordinating our steps with our breathing.

Sometimes the activity of walking meditation helps release repressed painful memories, allowing them to rise to the surface of our consciousness – though this may happen just as easily when we are practicing sitting meditation. Taking into consideration that our whole body stores memories and that walking meditation is a somatic as well as a mental and emotional activity, we can see the relationship between movement and the freeing of repressed or suppressed painful feelings. We need to be careful not to repress any of our emotions when they arise, whether they are caused by a current situation or as a result of old memories suddenly welling up into consciousness.

If we bottle up our anger and our pain, like frustration at being caught up in a traffic jam or the trauma of a past event, it will explode later, perhaps in a situation that has nothing to do with the cause. Walking meditation is an excellent technique for grounding painful emotions in the here and now of our life, because the act of mindful walking keeps our attention firmly in our body. Through the simple repeated actions of lifting one foot up and placing it down, the power of the painful emotions raging through our mind and body lessen until calm is restored.

Bringing meditation into our daily life also means being mindful to apply the remedies of reason, logic, and analysis to such situations, whether we are in formal meditation or not. In this way, we transform negative feelings rather than suppress them. So if painful or negative feelings from the past or present arise in walking meditation, then we can also practice insight meditation in order to better understand these feelings and let go of them. All things, even our most powerful emotions, are impermanent. With sitting meditation, we watch thoughts and feelings arise and pass. In walking meditation the act of lifting the foot and placing it down, the taking of one step followed by another, keeps us in touch with each unique moment of our life as it comes and goes.

practicing walking meditation

In this meditation your only concern is to lift one foot up slowly, move it forward, and place it down, followed by the other foot. With single-pointed concentration on this simple act, you let go of thoughts and preoccupation with a destination.

instructions for walking meditation

1   Have a clear idea of your walking path; between 10 and 20 meters is sufficient. This can be inside a room or outside in nature. Being in nature can substantially enrich the experience, but we need to be careful not to become distracted by what is happening around us.

2   Stand for a few minutes in calm meditation. Then start to walk slowly, being aware of picking up each foot and putting it down. Feel all the muscles and energies involved. Feel each part of the foot leave its contact with the ground and then reconnect. You can make each step fit in with each in- and out-breath if you like. The whole body should be relaxed and move freely. While you are walking, your arms should be folded gently over your abdomen or hanging loosely at your sides.

3   Become aware of your body and its movements, but don't be distracted by sensations or thoughts. Remember that you are not going anywhere or coming from anywhere, you are just walking. When you reach the turning place, pause for a few moments, then turn and pause for another few moments, being aware of simply standing.

4   Slowly walk on. If you become distracted or painful memories arise, stand for a few moments in calm meditation and watch the breath. Then continue with the walking meditation. You can practice walking meditation for as long as you like or alternate it with sitting meditation.

buddhist chanting

Many forms of vocal spiritual expression exist within all the religious traditions, often to invoke an altered state of consciousness in which God or another divine presence can be more readily experienced. These methods of vocal expression range from chanting and recitation to singing devotional prayers, mantras – words or syllables of power, usually Sanskrit – and songs. Within the different Buddhist traditions the forms of chanting vary somewhat according to individual cultural and doctrinal characteristics, but they all share certain clearly recognizable features. It is also generally assumed that chanting works on different levels according to the disposition, commitment, and ability of the chanter.

The sonorous expression of vocal sound – chanting – has been used to create an altered state of consciousness for centuries. In other words chanting has been used as a method of self-entrancement. The mind becomes free from mundane and worldly concerns, enabling the practitioner to view the perfection of the world and all things in it just as they are, without the overlay of conceptual thought and concerns of the ego. In Buddhist terminology, this is called transcending the world of duality or leaving behind the conventional view and how we usually perceive things in order to reach a nondual state. This ultimate view is how Buddhas, those who are enlightened, perceive. This ultimate view is also how things actually exist, interdependently and not in isolation from everything else.

Chanting involves repeating a word, sound, or phrase – or mantra, according to Buddhist terminology – as the meditation practice. After some time of repeating the same sounds we start to "become" the sound. In other words the firm hold of the ego and the personality loosens somewhat and we become as one with our mantra. Sound is composed of vibration, and whenever we chant, the sound resonates throughout our mind, body, and emotions.

The words and sounds used for Buddhist chanting have profound significance. These ancient (often Sanskrit) sounds represent fundamental qualities inherent in the universe, such as compassion or even the sound of the universe in motion. Thus it is not an intellectual meditation. We do not attempt to tease out a deeper meaning using analytical logic, but rather we surrender to the sound and allow the power of what it represents to permeate our consciousness, ideally accompanied by a deep sense of peace and well-being.

We also experience the silence between each individual chant, which gradually becomes a deep inner silence. Eventually we might reach a level of consciousness when each time the sound arises out of the silence it feels like original sound arising from out of the void. In this way we then feel connected to the essence of the universal life force itself and can feel for ourselves a deep connection with all that exists.

Although all the Buddhist traditions include forms of chanting, such as mantra recitation and the chanting of texts known as *sutras* (or *suttas*), we will look at two traditions in which chanting is the foremost practice. Pure Land Buddhism originated from the cult of Amitabha in China and Japan during the 13th century. Pure Land is primarily a devotional practice based on the assumption that we live in a degenerate age, so it is futile and arrogant to think we can attain liberation through our own efforts. Pure Land teaches that we can attain liberation only by letting go of our personal spiritual ambitions and surrendering to the infinite mercy and grace of Amitabha, the Buddha of Infinite Light.

pure land buddhist chanting

The practice involves faithfully chanting Amitabha's name and his mantra, which is called the Nembutsu, Namu-Amida-butsu. Pure Land devotees go around in their daily life continuously reciting the name of Amitabha or his mantra under their breath as well as formally chanting once or twice a day in front of a statue of Amitabha. Serious practitioners might undertake a meditation retreat where this chanting is their sole activity, and there are also Pure Land monks and nuns devoted to the practice.

The liberation for Pure Land Buddhists is rebirth into the Pure Land of Amitabha, known as the Western Paradise of Sukhavati. Sukhavati is described as the most beautiful place imaginable, with golden trees and ponds translucent like

crystal, surrounded by infinite numbers of lotus flowers. In Sukhavati all wishes and needs are automatically fulfilled through the compassion of Amitabha, who resides there. Unsurprisingly Sukhavati is also called the highest happiness.

However, Sukhavati is not just some kind of Buddhist heaven where you go when you die. The power of the chanting creates a Pure Land in the here and now. Committed practitioners, who chant almost continuously, describe how they live in a state of near bliss much of the time and see everyday objects as beautiful as they are in Sukhavati. One Pure Land nun says her mind is endlessly filled with the Pure Land; when she dreams she is automatically transported there, and when she moves around in daily life, she is walking on lotus flowers, as she would in Sukhavati. The power of chanting, combined with faith in Amitabha and belief in Sukhavati, enables Pure Land practitioners to experience something like a paradise here and now on earth.

nichiren shoshu chanting

Pure Land Buddhism is a small Buddhist school compared with the Nichiren Shoshu school, which also has chanting as a fundamental practice. Nichiren Shoshu is one of the most popular traditions in the West, with several famous adherents, such as Tina Turner, giving the school a high profile. Nichiren appears rather un-Buddhist at first glance, beause newcomers are encouraged to chant for whatever they want, which is usually material and sensual gratification. However, the philosophy says that if people achieve material success through the power of their chanting, then they will turn to more spiritual pursuits, firmly convinced of the spiritual potency of chanting. In this way practitioners progress from worldly desires toward the desire for spiritual fulfillment and ultimately nirvana. However, it is assumed that through the power of chanting, practitioners eventually develop spiritually until they are beyond desire altogether.

The lay organization of Nichiren, called the Soka Gakkai, has many international members, with the majority in Japan, where it originated. Coordinated from national headquarters, local groups meet regularly for group chanting, though practitioners are expected to chant twice daily. Each practitioner is given a copy of the Dai Gohonzon, which is the mantra Namu-myoho-renge-kyo, written in the form of a mandala by the founder, the 13th-century priest Nichiren Daishonin.

Practitioners develop faith in the power of Gohonzon in a similar way that Pure Land practitioners develop faith in Sukhavati. They chant Namu-myoho-renge-kyo in front of their Gohonzon twice a day with a firm idea of something they want, actually chanting for the fulfillment of their desires. Chanting extracts from and studying the Lotus Sutra, one of the teachings of the Buddha, supplements the main chanting practice of Namu-myoho-renge-kyo.

chanting a prayer to tara

Tara is a Tibetan Buddhist deity who is a manifestation of the wisdom, love, compassion, and skillful activity of all the Buddhas. Chanting this simple prayer to Tara, together with her mantra, opens our heart to the enlightened qualities that she represents.

instructions for chanting a prayer to tara

1 Sit quietly in the meditation posture and spend a few minutes watching the breath in calm meditation. You might want to have a picture or statue of Tara in front of you or you can simply visualize her. Contemplate her enlightened qualities and reflect on the benefits of chanting this prayer in praise of Tara. You can also make requests to Tara such as wishing for health, happiness, and so on.

2 Now chant Tara's mantra, *Om Tare Tuttare Ture Soha*, for a few minutes or 21 times, an auspicious number in Tibetan Buddhist practice. Really feel how these ancient spiritual words resonate in the core of your being. As you chant the prayer, visualize rainbow-like rays of light flowing from Tara's heart into your own, purifying yourself and all beings.

__Om__, I and all prostrate to the liberator, the fully realized, transcendent subduer.
I prostrate to the glorious mother who liberates with __tare__;
You are the mother who eliminates all fears with __tuttare__;
You are the mother who grants all success with __ture__;
To __soha__ and the other syllables we offer the greatest homage.

3 Chant the prayer as long as you like. When you finish chanting, visualize Tara dissolving into you. You then become one with her holy body, speech, and mind.

4 Spend a few minutes in calm meditation experiencing the effects of chanting and feeling that you have received Tara's blessings.

christian chanting

The word "chant" can conjure up all kinds of otherworldly associations such as enchantment, mysticism, magical ritual, and incantation, and chanting as a spiritual practice exists throughout the different countries of the world. Each kind of chant has its own musical character, form of expression, and cultural heritage. In addition to the Buddhist chants already described, there are Jewish, Muslim, African, and others from non-Christian cultures. In Christianity there is Armenian, Coptic, Georgian, Byzantine, Celtic, Iberian, and others too numerous to mention. However, the first written records of Christian chants, from about 900 A.D., are of what became known as Gregorian chants.

even today gregorian chants convey a
sense of mystery and spiritual purity that
transcend different times and fashions

Originally monks chanted the Latin Psalms as part of their liturgy, tapping into an ancient sacred ritual whose very sound could transport them and their listeners into a mystical experience. We often still feel Gregorian chanting evokes another realm of existence, and the contemporary popular revival of Gregorian chants and plainsong are a testimony to their enduring appeal. Even today Gregorian chants convey a sense of mystery and spiritual purity that transcend different times and fashions.

One reason why Gregorian chants remain mysterious is that they were designed mostly to be sung by an exclusive group of singers within a monastic choir. Thus most people experience the chants as listeners rather than as performers. However, because of the power of the chanting to evoke a spiritual response in the listener, the audience was deemed to be participating in the religious ceremony, albeit on an inactive level. Nonetheless, the chanting maintains a distance between a small esoteric group of spiritually developed initiates who perform for the benefit of a larger, mainly passive audience. Thus the mystical experience we encounter happens to us rather than as a result of our own action. In ancient times this illustrated the distance that was perceived between the congregation and God. Believing God to be unapproachably holy, priests and monks served as divine intermediaries for the congregants. In modern times it reflects our culture of passivity where we turn on the CD player, or the television, or go to a concert, often without even thinking of participating.

Elements within the musical form of Gregorian chanting reinforce the mystical experience in the listener. The chants are all sung in unison, which means all the singers sing exactly the same melody at exactly the same time. This produces a powerful and distinctive musical tone that invites the listener to participate vicariously, giving direct access to the music, which neither classical nor popular music achieves. Since only one pitch is sounding at any one time, we can hear the relationship between the pitches as the chant progresses, and it is in these relationships that we find the inner meaning.

In the Middle Ages, Gregorian chants were considered the music of the angels, and we can still hear this angelic and heavenly quality today, even if we are only listening to a CD. If we actually go to a concert in a cathedral and shut our eyes for a moment, we can easily still believe the music comes from the divine spheres. The music of the chant affects us on many levels. Because the words are in Latin most people can't understand on a rational level what is being sung, but on a nonverbal level the words themselves transcend meaning, often stimulating feelings of awe, reverence, and joy. Yet we remain aware that the words are religious, taken from the Psalms or the Catholic Mass. This facilitates our experience of communing with God, because we have gone beyond language to a deeper place within ourselves.

We might feel or sense that the Gregorian chant fulfills some ancient commitment to perform a sacred ritual, which in fact reflects its original use. Gregorian chants were originally sung as part of the Roman Catholic Mass and the music contributes to the atmosphere of liturgy. And as liturgy facilitates the spiritual ascent of the congregation, the mystique and beauty of Gregorian chanting helps guide the spirit toward the mystical and higher spiritual planes. In this way, we can understand why the singers were a small select group – the inner conviction and spiritual realization that came through their chanting needed to be of the most profound nature to guide the spirits of the congregation nearer to God.

an aid to meditation

Gregorian chants were historically used as Christian liturgy, where they were sung in the churches and cathedrals of the large cities, but were also used as an aid to the meditative monastic life. Some monks therefore lived in the cities, inevitably caught up in the worldly life to some degree, helping serve the larger spiritual needs of the congregations by performing the Gregorian chants each Sunday. Other monastics fled the crowded cities and contact with anything worldly to devote themselves to a life of meditation, craving solitude and peace in their desire to be at one with God. These hermit-like monastics sung the Gregorian chants as a way to facilitate a personal communion with God.

benedictine order

Around 540 A.D. a monk, Benedict, formed one of the first monastic communities in Europe. Benedict's Rule eventually became the model for other monastic communities because it successfully redressed these two extremes of worldly involvement and isolation. The communities collectively became known as the Benedictine Order and fundamental to their existence were the set periods of Gregorian chanting, which regulated their daily life. Thus Gregorian chants united the monks in communal worship at specific times of the day, but everyone had freedom for periods of personal meditation when chanting was often used as part of each individual's meditation practice.

Performing the Christian liturgy and individual monastic meditative singing of Gregorian chants kept this practice in the hands of the esoteric few. However, the congregation was not excluded from its own praise of God, and everyone was invited to join in the singing of hymns. The word "hymn" means to praise or to laud, and originally it was used as a verb as much as a noun. The original hymning was a kind of reiterative intonation of a praise word that is very close to chanting rather than the style of singing hymns today.

One of the early hymns familiar to all Christians was a unique form called the Hymn of All Creation. This is an original song of praise sung by all created things to their Creator, each praising God in its own peculiar way. The sun radiates its light, the storm thunders, each living creature cries aloud in praise, and humans chant, or sing, with words or without, or make sounds, each in their own way, praising the Creator who made them. Some of the ancient examples are both richly poetic and lyrical, the personal expressions of praise from the lay community inspired no doubt by the Gregorian chants of the monks.

practicing the gregorian chant

Since Gregorian chants and plainsong were originally sung by a group, it is appropriate here to make listening, rather than chanting, the main feature of this meditation. Obtain a recording of Gregorian chants. Because of their contemporary revival and popularity, a wide range is now available, such as those by the mystic Hildegard of Bingen. Alternatively, attend a recital in a cathedral and practice the meditation in the religious atmosphere where the Gregorian chants were originally performed.

instructions for gregorian chant meditation

1 Spend some moments connecting with your inner silence by watching the breath in calm meditation.

2 When the Gregorian chants commence, listen to the sound and allow it to completely envelop all your senses. Try to feel it in the core of your being. Reflect that over the centuries many people have used Gregorian chants as a way to commune with God. Observe your response to the sound. Feel that this experience is helping you connect with the divine and surrender to it completely.

3 When you finish listening, spend some moments appreciating your rarefied inner space and closeness to the divine before you move on.

hindu chakra
meditation

The main form of Hindu Chakra meditation is known as the Hindu Kundalini Yoga Chakra system. There are similarities to the Buddhist channel-wheel system described on pages 45–46, but the differences are important and vital to understanding the two separate systems. The Buddhist system was adapted from the much older Hindu, alongside other ancient Indian practices such as tantra. However, both share a profoundly ultimate nature that is experiential. What is described here is a simple conceptual overview.

The idea of a subtle body with three main channels like psychic nerves, called *nadis*, and several channel wheels, called chakras, are all present in this system with some differences from the Buddhist. The main channel is called the Sushumna and extends from the base of the spine near the second vertebra to the cranial fissure at the crown of the skull, known as the Brahmarandhra. It is described as being red like fire and a thousand times thinner than a human hair. This conveys the idea that these channels are of a subtle psychic nature rather than having a gross physical existence.

The two main subsidiary channels lie on either side of the Sushumna. On the left is the Ida, which means channel of comfort, and which carries the white, cooling energies of the moon. On the right is the Pingala, which means reddish brown channel, which carries the red heating energies of the sun. In the male, these two channels arise in the left and right testicles; in the female they arise in the right and left ovaries. The two subsidiary channels ascend alongside the central channel with no space between, until they reach the crown of the head. Just below the crown, they arch over and descend to the left and right nostrils.

At certain points up the body the two subsidiary channels cross over the central channel, making knots. This occurs at the six chakras along the central channel, but the most important are said to be the base, or muladhara chakra, the heart, or anahata chakra, and the forehead, or ajna chakra. These knots are likened to the meeting of the sacred rivers of India with the River Ganges likened to the Pingala, the River Yamuna to the Ida, and the hidden underground River Sarasvati to the Sushumna.

The main meditation, or yogic practice, that works with these energies is called pranayama, which means breath extension. As the name suggests, pranayama involves special techniques of inhalation, breath retention, and exhalation to

control and regulate the subtle "winds" that travel in these channels. The ultimate purpose is to arouse Kundalini Shakti, who is personified as a goddess coiled up in three and a half coils as a snake at the base of the central channel. She represents the ego or individual self. In normal conscious life, Kundalini is asleep with her head blocking the door of the central channel, so the chakras remain dormant.

awakening kundalini

Through the practice of pranayama, the Kundalini Yoga, the goddess Kundalini awakens and begins to turn inward. This is equated with the beginning of the dissolution of the ego, the individual self, and the absorption into the Higher Self, or atman. Kundalini then enters and ascends the central channel, finally merging with her consort Shiva in the thousand-petaled lotus, known as sahasrara padma, of the crown chakra at the top of the head. The level of bliss as Kundalini ascends the central channel and opens the chakras is said to be a hundred times more blissful than the temporary bliss of sexual orgasm. The psychic channels that carry the subtle winds of sexual orgasm momentarily enter the mouth of the central channel, so the bliss of Kundalini rising is said to be indescribable.

The six chakras are each like a lotus flower and have a varying number of petals, making a total of 50. Each petal is sealed with a Sanskrit syllable, reflecting the 50 letters of the Sanskrit alphabet, and each syllable is also a mantra of Kundalini. The center of each lotus also bears the symbol of a presiding deity, a goddess, an animal, an element shape, a color, and a seed-syllable called a *bija*. The six chakras represent the six realms of existence, or *lokas*.

At the base of the central channel, in the perineum, lies the muladhara chakra, which contains the sleeping Kundalini goddess serpent. The muladhara chakra has four petals and bears the yellow square of the earth element. Inside the square are a downward-pointing triangle, enclosing the syllable lam of the earth element, and a golden Shiva lingam (symbolizing the phallus), which Kundalini is coiled around. The presiding deity is Ganesha, the goddess is Dakini Shakti, and the animal is an elephant.

this is in the pure realm where kundalini and shiva unite, in the culmination of kundalini yoga achieved by only the most advanced and pure yogis of this tradition

Above this, in the pubic region, is the svadhisthana chakra with six red petals, bearing a white lunar crescent and the syllable vam of the water element. The presiding deity is Brahma, the goddess is Rakini, and the animal is a makara, a mythical sea monster like a crocodile. At the navel is the manipura chakra with 10 blue-gray petals bearing a red triangle and the syllable ram of the fire element. The presiding deity is Vishnu, the goddess is Lakshmi, and the animal a ram. At the heart is the anahata chakra with 12 red petals, bearing a blue-black six-pointed star and the syllable yam of the air, or wind element. The presiding deity is Rudra, the goddess is Kakini, and the animal is a deer.

At the throat is the vishuddha chakra with 16 purple petals, bearing a white circle resembling the full moon and the syllable ham of the space element within a downward-pointing triangle. The presiding deity is Sadashiva, the goddess is Shakini, and the animal is an elephant or a swan. At the center of the forehead between the eyebrows, a point sometimes called the "third eye," is the ajna chakra with two gray or white petals, symbolizing the two subsidiary channels, bearing a pure white circle and the syllable om, symbolizing the subtle essence of consciousness, enclosed in a downward-pointing triangle. The ajna chakra is sealed with this subtle essence of consciousness because it is here that the two subsidiary channels meet and descend toward the nostrils. The presiding deity is the Paramshiva, the goddess is Hakini, and the animal is a swan.

At the crown of the head is the seventh chakra, the sahasrara padma, or thousand-petaled lotus, which arises at the end of the central channel. This is in the pure realm where Kundalini and Shiva unite, in the culmination of Kundalini Yoga achieved by only the most advanced and pure yogis of this tradition. The thousand petals are pink or white and bear the 50 Sanskrit syllables in 20 radiating circles of lotus petals.

meditating on the hindu chakras

Kundalini Yoga is an advanced meditation practice unsuitable for beginners, so this simple meditation on the chakras, or energy centers, is a good place to start, and a useful prerequisite for Kundalini Yoga itself. There is much more to be learned, and the interested reader can find suitable books in the bibliography.

instructions for meditating on the hindu chakras

1   Start with watching the breath in calm meditation until the mind is calm and clear.

2   Look at the picture of the channels and chakras on page 63. Try to remember as many details as you can. Then visualize the whole chakra system. Don't worry if you can't remember everything. There is plenty of detail, and it will take time and repeated practice to visualize it all. Start with trying to remember the number and location of the chakras.

3   Open your eyes and focus on the muladhara chakra (in the next meditation session take the svadisthana chakra, and so on). Close your eyes and visualize the muladhara chakra with as many details as you can. Reflect upon the deities, elements, and other characteristics ascribed to the chakra. Allow the symbolism to just rest in your mind. After some time unconscious associations will arise, which may deepen your understanding.

4   Finish with some minutes of calm meditation to clear the mind.

the western
esoteric tradition

One of the Western esoteric traditions, the Kabbalah, is part of the ancient mystical tradition of the Hebrews. There are three primary Hebrew literatures – the Books of Law and the Prophets (commonly known as the Biblical Old Testament), the Talmud, which is composed of commentaries on these teachings, and the Kabbalah, which is the received wisdom and tradition of mystical knowledge believed to come from God. Tradition states that ignorant men may profit from the first, learned men from the second, but only the wise meditate upon the third.

Kabbalah also incorporates Esoteric Christianity, which arose from two spiritual communities, the Essenes and the Gnostics. Jesus was recognized as having enormous spiritual potential after speaking in the Temple at the age of 12. Some sources claim that afterward Jesus was sent to the Essenian community near the Dead Sea to train in the mystical tradition, remaining there until he came to John for baptism in the River Jordan. The esoteric mystic aspect of Christianity was eventually driven underground by mainstream exoteric Christianity.

over the centuries the ancient hebraic

wisdom was supplemented by alchemy

and astrology, so the kabbalah is rich

in mystical symbolism

The Mystical Kabbalah is sometimes called the Dharma or Yoga of the West, both Eastern terms, so we can see it as valid a spiritual tradition as Buddhism, Hinduism, Sufism, or Islam. Over the centuries the ancient Hebraic wisdom was supplemented by alchemy and astrology, so Kabbalah is rich in mystical symbolism. Everything of the Kabbalah and all the meditation practices are contained in its foremost symbol, Ets Chayyim, or the Tree of Life.

The Tree of Life consists of 10 spheres of divine attributes, the Ten Holy Sefirot, arranged over three pillars: the right-hand Pillar of Mercy, the central Pillar of Equilibrium, and the left-hand Pillar of Severity. These are connected by lines called the 32 Paths of the Divine Emanations. If we look at the Tree of Life, we observe that there are only 22 paths, but the Ten Sefirot are regarded as paths themselves. The Ten Sefirot are associated with the Ten Commandments. The number 22 is also the number of letters of the Hebrew alphabet, and each of the 22 paths after the first 10 of the Sefirot is associated with a Hebrew letter and also the 22 Tarot trump cards. We can see from these relations how complex a symbol the Tree of Life is and how a student requires a teacher to initiate her or him into the mysteries of the Kabbalah.

Further symbolic associations are also included, with the 12 signs of the zodiac, the seven planets, and the four elements. This makes a total of 23 symbols to fit onto 22 paths. Because we live on the physical plane, the element earth does not appear on the tree. The remaining 22 symbols, when correctly placed upon the tree, are found to correspond with the 22 Tarot trump cards, every symbol enriching one another and providing keys to understanding esoteric astrology and Tarot divination.

Higher levels of understanding the symbolism exist, if we know how to find them, together with further insight into the relationships between the Sefirot and the paths. We might wonder why much of the meaning is hidden from the casual observer, but the deeper levels of meaning are deliberately obscure to protect the esoteric knowledge from misuse by the casual spiritual shopper. The wisdom in the secret meaning is thereby kept hidden for those initiates and adepts to use in the way the Mystical Kabbalah has always required.

However, the interested reader can benefit from using the Tree of Life in meditation. The tree is a composite symbol that represents the cosmos and the soul of man in relation to the cosmos. Each Sefirah represents a phase of evolution and collectively they are called the Ten Holy Emanations. The Paths represent phases of subjective consciousness by which the soul gradually understands its relation to the cosmos. They can be fully understood only in relation to each other, not in isolation.

the ten sefirot

The first Sefirah, Keter, crystallizes out of the limitless light of the unformed universe; thus Keter is a condition of pure becoming. Keter means crown, which is worn above the head, and Keter, therefore, represents a higher level of consciousness beyond incarnation. Keter also means union with God, or enlightenment, the innermost spiritual essence from which all manifestation must spring. As Keter crystallizes from limitless light, so Chokhmah crystallizes from Keter. Chokhmah means wisdom, archetypal male or Supernal (celestial) Father and positive energy. It is the Illuminating Intelligence and a primary dynamic force in the universe, urging toward manifestation. Yet Chokhmah is before form, the pure impulse of dynamic creation, containing the potential to assume any form.

Binah crystallizes out of Chokhmah and means understanding. Binah is called the Sanctifying Intelligence and is the archetypal female, the Great Mother, both fertile and barren. Binah is stabilizing energy, the female potency of the universe, and the crystallization of the male dynamic creative impulse into form. Yet inherent in the birth of form are the seeds of death. She is the primordial root of matter, the destroyer of the force of energy. From Binah crystallizes Chesed, the loving father, protector, and preserver, the sphere of Jupiter. Chesed means mercy and represents the concretion of the abstract, the formulation of archetypal ideas. Chesed is called the Cohesive Intelligence, the creative energy of organized force, and the practical application of ideas.

Gevurah crystallizes from Chesed and means power and strength, like its image of the king going to war. Gevurah is the destroyer, the lord of fear and severity, and balances the qualities of Chesed. Gevurah is the sphere of Mars and called the Radical Intelligence, representing the release of force in activity. Tiferet crystallizes from Gevurah and lies at the center of the tree, representing the center and power of equilibrium. Tiferet means beauty and is the Son to Keter, the Father, God made manifest in form, the true illuminated vision. Tiferet is the child and the sacrificed God, like Jesus, the redeemer and is called the Mediating Intelligence, the regenerative aspect of religion.

tiferet means beauty and is
the son to keter, the father, god
made manifest in form, the true
illuminated vision

Netzach crystallizes from Tiferet, is the sphere of Venus, and means victory. Netzach represents the instincts, the emotions, and the arts, and is called the Occult Intelligence. Netzach is the higher aspect of elemental forces, the practical, creative force expressed in nature. Netzach is the mystical artistic impulse balancing the scientific impulse of Hod. Hod crystallizes from Netzach, represents astral consciousness, and means glory. Hod is the formulation of forms, the intellectual aspect of magic, and the sphere of Mercury. Hod is called the Perfect Intelligence and represents power in equilibrium. Hod designs, constrains, limits, and formulates; the sacrifice of fluidity and flexibility gives direction and control.

Yesod crystallizes from Hod and means foundation, strength, and stability, yet also fluidity. Yesod is called the Pure Intelligence and is the receptacle of the emanations of the other Sefirot, purifying and refining them. Yesod is the sphere of the Moon and illusion and corresponds to psychic consciousness and the unconscious mind. Malkhut crystallizes from Yesod, means the Kingdom, and is the nadir of evolution. Malkhut is the sphere of the Earth and form and brain consciousness. Malkhut gives stability and coherence to the final level of manifestation, is called the Resplendent Intelligence, and represents action on the physical plane.

meditating on the tree of life

When we view the Tree of Life in the picture below, we are viewing it as a reflection of ourselves. When we meditate on the Tree as a blueprint of ourselves, the mirror image is reversed so left-hand becomes right, and right becomes left.

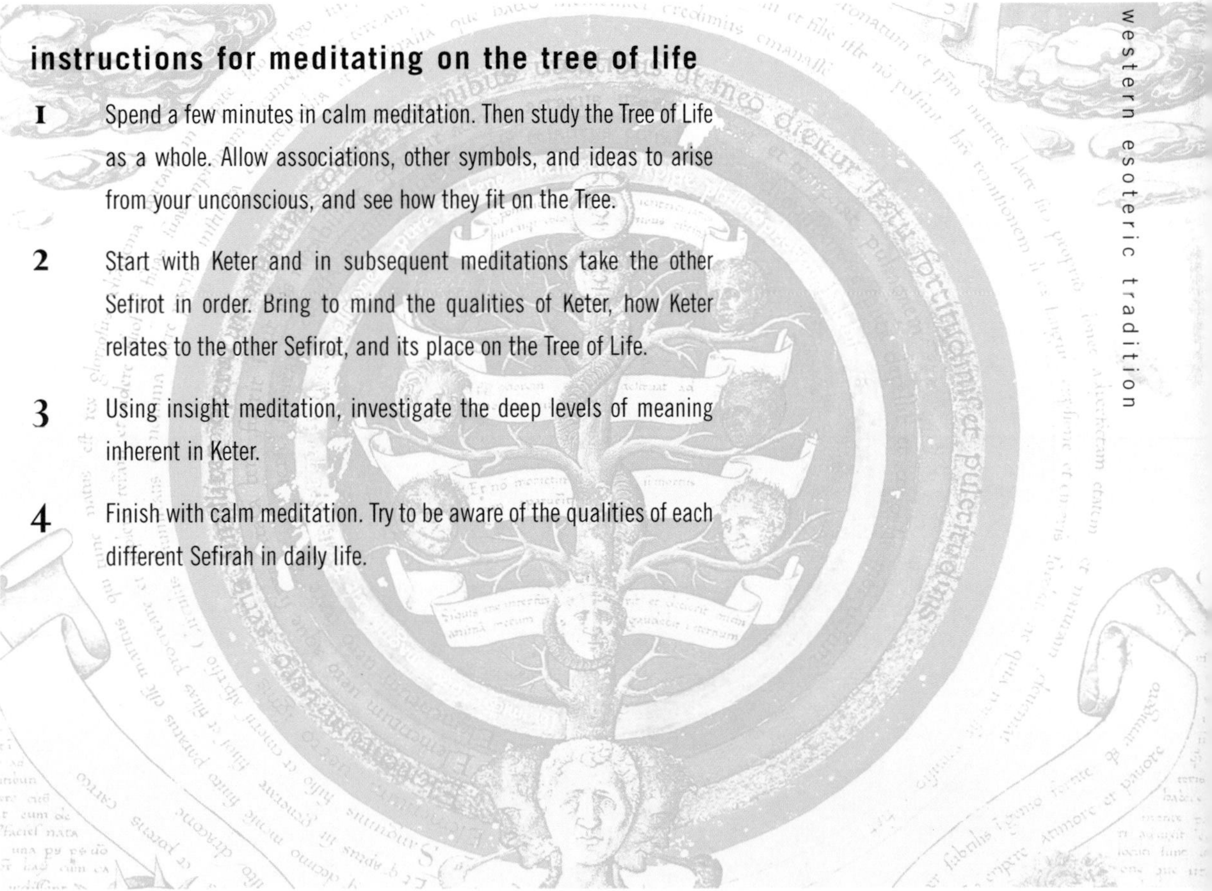

instructions for meditating on the tree of life

I   Spend a few minutes in calm meditation. Then study the Tree of Life as a whole. Allow associations, other symbols, and ideas to arise from your unconscious, and see how they fit on the Tree.

2   Start with Keter and in subsequent meditations take the other Sefirot in order. Bring to mind the qualities of Keter, how Keter relates to the other Sefirot, and its place on the Tree of Life.

3   Using insight meditation, investigate the deep levels of meaning inherent in Keter.

4   Finish with calm meditation. Try to be aware of the qualities of each different Sefirah in daily life.

transcendental
meditation

Transcendental Meditation is essentially thousands of years old but first came to the West in 1958 with the original visit of the Indian monk and physicist Maharishi Mahesh Yogi. Maharishi adapted the technique of Transcendental Meditation (TM) from the ancient Sanskrit Vedas, the sacred Indian texts, for the purpose of helping people unfold the full potential of their lives. One reason for its nearly instant popularity was the guru-disciple relationship between Maharishi and the Beatles, who had encountered Maharishi when they traveled to India on a spiritual quest. The high media profile of the pop group ensured that TM received a lot of free publicity.

Since the Beatles' heyday and the 1960s ethos, when meditation was an indispensable accessory to the hippie lifestyle, many people from all walks of life have taken up TM, as it has now become familiarly known. Though the actual meditation practice shares some similarities with other sitting meditations, TM is presented without a spiritual belief system or philosophy and more as a complementary therapy, relaxation technique, and for stress management. This formula attracts people who might feel skeptical or afraid of meditation that is encapsulated in an ethical or religious framework.

There are local Transcendental Meditation centers as well as national centers in many countries around the world. People who decide to practice TM are taught the meditation by teachers exclusively trained by Maharishi. This keeps the lineage of the tradition pure and ensures that the standard of training remains constant. As well as teaching meditation, various centers and experienced individual TM practitioners have engaged in scientific and medical research to demonstrate the power of meditation in helping prevent and treat illness and disease. The results of this research demonstrate that by dissolving stress and tension, meditation helps the mind, body, and spirit regenerate, bringing about both healing and the potential to realize more in life.

Transcendental Meditation is learned within a systematic course of instruction, consisting of a seven-step program. The first three sessions are introductory and explain the history and background of TM, and the next four are instructions on the meditation technique itself. Standards and method of instruction are universal to all the centers, so every student is taught the same material in the same way. It is emphasized that no special ability is required, that indeed anyone can learn and practice TM. The Transcendental Meditation organization is a charity and runs several schools where children are taught meditation. These children seem to benefit from meditating, which is reflected in their enhanced learning ability, especially in creative subjects such as poetry.

Once prospective students have attended an introductory presentation, if they decide to proceed with learning the meditation, they sign up for instruction sessions. Students are then taught the meditation technique under the guidance and advice of a TM teacher. The meditation consists of working with a mantra, in this instance one of a number of words derived from the Vedas by Maharishi. Each student is given the mantra that best suits his or her character and disposition, and this special word is kept secret to retain its efficacy. Because students do not know the meaning of their mantra, they meditate using the sound of the word only. No concentration is involved, so by using the sound of the mantra the practitioner can access deeper levels of the mind and rest in the level of consciousness before thought arises.

After practitioners complete the course, it is recommended that they meditate twice a day for 20 minutes each session, first thing in the morning and late afternoon or evening. Advanced courses exist for those who wish to learn more. There is a charge for learning the meditation technique, and it is emphasized that this must be taught by a TM teacher and not learned from a book.

buddhist
visualization

Visualization is used in several of the Buddhist practices and meditations in the different Buddhist traditions, but reaches the level of an art form in Tibetan Buddhist tantra, which is explored in a later chapter. Other Buddhist visualizations include an alternative way to develop single-pointed concentration by visualizing an image of Shakyamuni Buddha as the focus of our attention. If we alternate between different objects of meditation such as watching the breath and visualizing the Buddha, this helps to keep the mind fresh and alert. As soon as the mind becomes dull from using one meditation object, we can switch to the other. Visualizing the Buddha generates merit and *bodhicitta*, the mind that seeks enlightenment.

We can also use visualization to enhance analytical meditation, such as when we practice death meditation. Reflecting upon our mortality and the fact that we know neither the time nor the circumstances of our death brings one level of understanding, but if we think of our body as a corpse, this brings the reality of our inevitable death to a much deeper level. We can extend the visualization to include our friends and family grieving at our funeral, and by doing so realize how precious our brief and uncertain life is. We can also remember to appreciate our friends and family and reflect that the love and friendship they freely give us will one day be cut short by death. Meditating on the certainty of death paradoxically allows us to live our lives more fully, because we remain aware of the precious and impermanent nature of our life.

The devotional practices of Buddhism are also substantially enriched by visualization. These include the chanting, singing, or recitation of prayers and mantras, and performing prostrations, or bowing down in front of an image of Buddha. Sometimes those of us from Western cultures find the idea of devotional practices a bit difficult. For example, since the Bible forbids bowing down in front of graven images or idols, some of us from Christian backgrounds may be uncomfortable bowing down before Buddha. However, when we understand that we are not bowing down to an external Buddha image, even though we often perform prostrations in front of such an image, but that our prostrations are honoring and cultivating our own potential for enlightenment, we find this practice easier. If we visualize one of the forms of Buddha as we do prostrations, we reinforce our motivation to attain enlightenment.

The devotional prayers of Buddhism often include descriptions of offerings we are making to the Buddha, and obviously this becomes a much stronger practice if we visualize the offerings we are mentally or physically making. Offerings traditionally include flowers, incense, candles, and small bowls of water. When we recite prayers that include offerings, we can visualize these offerings, making them as beautiful as possible because we are offering them to Buddha. One of the main prayers recited at the beginning of most Tibetan Buddhist practices is called Offering the Mandala, which involves mentally transforming everything in the universe into a pure realm and offering this to the Buddha, the Dharma, or his teachings, and the Sangha, or spiritual community.

We visualize the whole universe in miniature in the space directly in front of us, and then visualize it transformed into a pure realm. Everything in a pure realm – the people, the objects, and even the whole environment – is beautiful and blissful; in pure realms everything makes the mind peaceful and joyful. We use our imagination and visualization to create this paradisaical pure realm and then we offer it to the Buddha, Dharma, and Sangha. Try to offer the gift without attachment to any part of it and imagine that it is received with great pleasure and appreciation.

visualizing the breath meditation

If the exercise above sounds like a rather daunting task, there are simpler visualization practices we can begin with. When we are watching the breath in calm meditation, we can incorporate visualizing our breath for some of the time, perhaps three inhalations and three exhalations. As we breathe in, we visualize the air as pure white light, and we say to ourselves that we are breathing in the love, wisdom, and compassion of the Buddhas. As we breathe out, we visualize the air as black smoke, and we say to ourselves that we are breathing out our anger, hatred, and self-cherishing or selfishness. This easy practice is surprisingly powerful for developing positive qualities and letting go of negative ones. It also transforms our basic practice of watching the breath into a purification meditation.

Another purification Buddhist meditation using visualization is the Body of Light meditation. This is good for generating peace, happiness, and harmony, promoting relaxation, and helping us become aware of areas of stress and tension in our body. We can include this meditation during the middle of a session of watching the breath in calm meditation, especially if we are feeling depressed or lethargic. We visualize a sphere of white light in the space above our head and see it as radiant and vibrant as possible. During the visualization, feel that the light represents universal love and wisdom and then visualize the light descending into the top of the head and traveling down to the heart. Feel blessed by the light.

After some time we visualize the light expanding to fill our whole body, until every part feels suffused with white light. We imagine that all our negative emotions have been transformed into positive qualities, and that we are full of love, compassion, and wisdom. We feel at one with the universe, and that everything is perfect just as it is here and now. Allow the visualized light to fade and return to watching the breath. This is a useful practice if we have recently experienced a negative interaction with someone, because the visualized light is most effective in restoring a sense of purified inner space.

practicing meditation on loving-kindness
This gentle and healing meditation is fundamental to all Buddhist traditions and uses visualization to explore our interconnectedness with all people, animals, insects, and other life forms as well as the whole environment.

instructions for meditation on loving-kindness

I Spend some time in calm meditation, watching the breath and discovering in your heart a warm, caring feeling toward all life.

2 Now develop loving-kindness toward your self. Visualize yourself as a human being with faults and good qualities – but someone who has the right to find happiness. Developing loving-kindness toward yourself is the first step to developing loving-kindness toward others. Silently say, "May I live in safety. May I experience mental happiness, peace and joy, physical happiness and health. May my daily life go well, with no difficulties."

3 After a few minutes visualize someone who has helped you. Repeat the phrases using that person's name while visualizing the person and remembering his or her great kindness toward you. Feel loving-kindness toward that person.

4 Then include a good friend and repeat the phrases and the visualization accordingly. Next include someone toward whom you have no strong feelings. Remind yourself that this person has the right to live life free from suffering and find happiness just like you.

5 Now include someone who has harmed you or for whom you have negative feelings. The person is not the action and you do not have to condone the negative behavior. Contemplate that people who behave badly often experience much suffering, so offering them loving-kindness might help.

6 Finally, include all beings everywhere and visualize yourself in the middle of a crowd containing all beings. Reflect on how we are all interdependent with each other and extend loving-kindness to all. Finish with some moments of watching the breath and dedicate any merit from this meditation toward the happiness of all beings.

haiku poetry

Religious poetry from all historical periods and different cultures can be found that expresses the poet's spiritual struggles, devotion to a particular God, or glorying in God's creation. The form of the poetry varies widely, including sonnets, free verse, odes, and prose poems, and often does not reflect the poet's spiritual attainments or discipline. So though the poet's expression, the poem, may be well crafted, beautiful, and poignant, and reflect his or her deep spiritual understanding, the form of the composition is largely incidental.

There is one notable exception: the Japanese poet Matsuo Basho, who wrote poetry in the classical Japanese style known as haiku, or *hokku,* as it was called in his time. Haiku is the shortest classical poetic form in Japanese poetry, and its brevity and formal structure require huge discipline to write well. A haiku poem must be exactly 17 syllables over three lines of five, then seven, then five. A haiku poet trains for years to learn how to convey meaning succinctly in such a formal and short form. Japanese Zen Buddhism is also known for its short, sharp aphorisms and stringent meditations, and Basho somehow combines the two disciplines in extraordinary spiritual poetry, where the form of the poem, the haiku, is essential to convey the profound meaning.

a haiku poet trains for years to learn how to convey meaning succinctly in such a formal and short form

Basho was born in 1644 in the city of Ueno and at age nine entered the service of the city's ruling family as a page. His duties largely consisted of studying with the son and heir, Yoshitada, whose delicate health inclined him to literary subjects, so Basho had an early opportunity to learn the art of poetry. When Yoshitada died at only 25 years of age, Basho ran away to Kyoto to pursue his studies. After five years in Kyoto he had already established his reputation as a haiku poet and moved to the city of Edo. By the age of 36, having had enough of the "floating world" of secular pleasures and society, he moved to an isolated house near the River Sumida, built for him by an admirer.

Shortly after moving he met the Zen priest Buccho and started to practice Zen meditation under Buccho's guidance. Basho's haiku poetry from this period reflects his spiritual anguish and internal suffering, and the poems are noticeably more mature in both style and content. Basho now wrote of how he saw the world

77

with a new vision, infused with the inner learning from meditation. Though the subject matter often remained rooted in nature and natural images, there is a strong metaphorical quality reflecting his inner spiritual state and journey.

Basho describes the process of haiku: "What is important is to keep our mind high in the world of true understanding and returning to the world of our daily experience to seek therein the truth of beauty." This reflects his spiritual understanding from years of deep meditation and severe self-scrutiny. Basho spent his remaining years traveling and writing haiku along the way and recording his travels in a mixture of prose and haiku. The most famous collection is called *The Narrow Road to the Deep North*, and even in the title we can see the inner journey reflected in the outer. Basho's most famous haiku follows (in translation the number of syllables and lines is lost):

Breaking the silence

Of an ancient pond,

A frog jumped into water —

A deep resonance.

Using Basho as an inspiration, we can write our own haiku out of the experience of our meditation, making the actual writing of the poem a form of meditation, too. It is not necessary to have previous experience of writing poetry, because we are not writing for an audience other than ourselves, nor are we trying to impress anyone with our poetic skill. If we think of the actual writing as a meditation as well as writing about our experiences in meditation, we realize there is no striving for anything other than authentic expression.

However, it is important to retain the discipline inherent in the haiku form, so each haiku must consist of 17 syllables in the five/seven/five three-line structure. We also use nature metaphors and natural images to reflect our inner space, our spiritual feelings, whether these are full of despair, joy, or are even neutral. There is no point trying to emulate the Japanese cultural style of the period when Basho was writing. Find a style that resonates with your own culture in the here and now. In this way the natural images will be drawn from a living nature that you can see, hear, and feel around you, not some mythologized idea of what nature might be.

The use of metaphor, using a word or phrase that says one thing to mean another, was refined by Basho to a very subtle level, which he described as a theory combining substance and essence. We don't need to be so sophisticated when we begin writing haiku, unless we want to, but we can try to use metaphors and similes to convey the inner and outer meanings. A simile compares a word or phrase to another word to convey the idea of likeness, rather than saying it *is* something as a metaphor does. We know willows don't paint eyebrows, but this is a poetic way to describe how the shadow of the willow falls on the cliff.

An example of metaphor:

A hanging willow
In beautiful green
Paints eyebrows
On the brow of a cliff.

An example of simile:

Separated we shall be
For ever, my friends,
Like the wild geese
Lost in the clouds.

writing haiku meditation

You can practice this meditation while sitting outside in the midst of nature or inside with a view of nature to get inspiration and ideas for images to use in your own haiku. Or you can sit inside as usual and use your imagination.

instructions for writing haiku meditation

1   Spend some minutes in calm meditation, watching the breath. Then invite images from nature to arise in your mind as a reflection of your inner state. Don't worry if nothing comes; just keep on watching the breath with an open mind.

2   Once a strong image has come, examine it by using analytical insight meditation. Use the insights, associations, and other images that arise to refine the idea until it reflects your mind state.

3   Write the image down, and start shaping it into your haiku poem.

4   Once the haiku is complete, spend some minutes in calm meditation to clear the mind. Finish by reading your haiku, out loud if you like, and see how it resonates with your inner state.

sufi dancing

Sufi spiritual practice is based on trying to awaken God not just in, but as, the practitioner and involves the whole person – mind, body, and spirit. In Christianity we try to experience God's presence in ourselves; in Sufi practice we try to experience God as ourselves. This intention gave rise to the practice of whirling, a religious ritual spinning dance that reflects the circular movement of everything in the universe, from the neutrons whirling around the nucleus in every atom to the planets revolving around the stars. The original Muslim Sufi priests who practiced this were called dervishes, a word meaning the doorway between our mundane world and the heavenly world. The sacred ritual of the Whirling Dervishes, called the *sema*, aims to awaken the divine presence manifesting within the practitioner.

This sacred ritual movement was introduced into the Turkish Mevlevi order by the mystical Sufi poet Jelaluddin Rumi more than 700 years ago. Whirling Dervishes, or *semazen*, wear tall, cone-shaped felt hats and wide white skirts that represent the tombstone of the ego and the ego's shroud, respectively. In the ceremony dervishes wear a black cloak, which, when removed, symbolizes being spiritually born to truth.

The practice of whirling starts with the arms crossed over the heart and the hands of each arm on the opposite shoulder. With the right toe placed on top of the left, the dervishes bow deeply to each other. As they rise from the bow, their feet uncross. The whirling then starts in a counterclockwise direction with the body's weight on the left foot, which is rotated with the right foot and used to

propel the body around, occasionally touching the ground to maintain balance. The axis they spin on is between the big toe of the left foot and the next toe.

The whirling gradually picks up speed, and when balance has been established the arms unfold, like an eagle spreading its wings. The right hand opens upward to the skies to receive God's blessings and the left hand turns downward to the earth in a gesture of bestowal. Whirling in synchronicity with the infinite spiraling of the cosmos yet with their feet anchored on the ground, they are transported into a state of ecstasy. Eventually they slow down to a stop and repeat their bow.

practicing the *dhikr*

The *dhikr* is similar to but easier than whirling. Only the head is rotated while repeating the *dhikr*, a sacred phrase in which the name of God is repeated.

instructions for practicing the *dhikr*

I   Sit in the meditation posture and relax the body while watching the breath for a few minutes.

2   Starting on an exhalation, turn the head in a half circle from the left shoulder, down to the left knee, past the right knee, and up to the right shoulder, then right up to the top. As you circle the head, repeat silently or aloud, "La ilaha" or "There is no other divinity."

3   On the inhalation, drop the head down toward the solar plexus. Then, without pausing, raise the head back up until the face is turned upward. As you move the head, repeat "illa 'llah" or "except God."

4   Holding the breath, turn the head toward the heart in the upper left of the chest, repeating the word "hu." This means him or he who is absent. Then repeat the sequence for as long as you wish.

5   When you wish to finish, spend some minutes in calm meditation, reflecting that the purpose of practicing the *dhikr* is to make God present and incorporates the whole mystery of the divine being that manifests in both the transcendent and immanent dimensions.

koan meditation

Koans are used together with zazen – an intensive sitting meditation in the Rinzai tradition of Zen Buddhism – as a method to attain enlightenment, known as *satori*. Koan and zazen are described as being the two handmaidens of Zen. The first is the eye and the other the foot. A koan, or *hwadu* in Korean, is a short cryptic statement rather than a riddle or a witty remark. Its object is to cause doubt to arise in the mind and take this doubt to its furthest limits. Koans were originally devised by the early great Zen masters out of compassion for their students to help them reach *satori*. However, they were aware that they were creating an artificial device because unless enlightenment arose from a person's own inner experience, it could not be totally authentic. True *satori* being so rare, however, meant koans were used to help the tradition stay alive. Their use preserved the inquiring mind that leads toward enlightenment. When koan and zazen are used correctly they help unfold the mind to ultimate truth.

Koan meditation originated in China and traveled to Japan and Korea, where it still remains a fundamental Zen practice. Koans are not designed to be understood intellectually, and working with questioning and doubt allows other faculties of the mind to come into play, beyond conceptual thought or intellect. By throwing themselves against the iron wall of the koan, students transcend the limits of logical, dualistic thought, and awaken to an inner sense, enabling them to see directly into how things truly exist.

a koan, or hwadu *in korean, is a short cryptic statement rather than a riddle or a witty remark*

Koans are often questions but there is no ultimate answer. The intention is for the student to keep questioning and through this realize that what he or she has so far accepted as "reality" or "truth" is not necessarily so – there are other ways of seeing. This continual inquiry takes the student to the limits of his or her intellectual capability, eventually breaking through to other levels of the mind, known as Zen consciousness on the way to full *satori*. Koans are not nonsensical and do have some meaning, but to work out the intellectual meaning is not the intention of Zen and not especially helpful.

Perhaps the most famous koan to reach the West is "What is the sound of one hand clapping?" This koan originated from the Zen master Hakuin, who used to hold up one hand and demand of his students to hear the sound of it. Of course a sound is heard only when two hands are clapped together and no sound can come from one hand alone. What Hakuin was doing was challenging our everyday experience founded upon an empirical, logical basis. Only by relinquishing this understanding can we open our mind to other levels. Until the mind can perceive a sound produced by one hand, it remains limited and buried in relativity.

Working with a koan in zazen is usually undertaken in a formal setting, such as a monastery or a meditation retreat and includes a weekly meeting, called a *sanzen*, with the Zen master. The master questions the students about their understanding of the koan and after a few sessions the students will have exhausted all conceptual views of the koan and feel trapped in a mental cul-de-sac. This deeply frustrating experience can lead almost to despair, but is in fact the true starting point of Zen. From then on the students' minds will begin to open to other levels of consciousness.

practicing the zen koan meditation "what is this?"

This koan is frequently used in Zen meditation retreats in the West. As you ask yourself the question it is helpful to change the significance of each word from time to time, so you might start by emphasizing "what," then move to "is" and finally "this." These subtle changes in the importance of each word to the overall koan become relevant when the question is repeated continuously.

instructions for zen koan meditation

1 Sit in the usual meditation posture and spend a few minutes watching the breath.

2 Start asking the question "What is this?" silently in your mind, over and over.

3 The question could be "Who is this?" but because we are trying to go beyond our usual sense of identity, "What is this?" helps us move beyond our sense of ego. Irritation will arise, but just keep questioning and let the feeling pass.

4 Keep questioning for as long as you can and when you finish, ask the question occasionally during your daily life.

tantra

There are two levels of practice in Buddhism, sutra and tantra, which exist because of the differing dispositions of practitioners. But all students of Buddhism spend some years on the sutra path, practicing meditation and developing basic Buddhist principles such as morality, compassion, and patience before thinking about whether to begin the tantric path. They will have gained some experiential understanding of the Buddhist concept of emptiness known as *sunyata*. This is the Buddhist philosophy that logically explains the lack of inherent existence of all phenomena, which means that all things exist interdependently. The tantric aspirant must also be committed to the *bodhisattva* ideal: the wish to become enlightened for the benefit of all sentient beings, not just for personal nirvana. Tantra is therefore an advanced practice for experienced Buddhists.

Tantra, or *vajrayana*, is known as the third turning of the wheel of Dharma. The first turning of the wheel of Dharma was Buddha's teachings during his lifetime and the initial commentaries, which are incorporated in Theravada Buddhism. The second turning refers to the later development of Mahayana Buddhism. The third turning is tantra, a further development of Mahayana Buddhism, drawn from and inspired by the ancient Indian Hindu tantras. The introduction of tantra into Tibet profoundly enriched the different schools of Tibetan Buddhism, and the term *vajrayana* takes its name from the *vajra*, or *dorje*, one of the sacred ritual objects used in tantric practice.

The practice of tantra opens the door to a magical and metaphysical realm rich in symbolism and ritual. The late British Buddhist author John Snelling said, "The aim of tantric practice is to transform one's body, speech, and mind into those of a fully enlightened Buddha by special yogic means." Tantra is also called "deity practice" and involves visualizing oneself as one of the many Tibetan Buddhist deities and reciting praises and prayers to that deity. The tantric practitioner thereby gains a profound experiential understanding of the symbolism and meaning encapsulated in the particular deity.

Tibetan Buddhist deities are either peaceful or wrathful. The smiling, benign, and otherworldly expressions on peaceful deities show how they embody the peace and tranquillity of enlightenment. Such deities include Chenrezig, the Bodhisattva of Compassion, who is also called Avalokiteshvara, with either four arms or a thousand arms, symbolizing his compassionate intention to alleviate the suffering of all beings. Green Tara, a popular female deity, is depicted with one foot outstretched, ready to jump up and help anyone requesting her assistance. Vajrasattva is the Bodhisattva of purification. The scriptures say that tantric meditation upon this deity eliminates our delusions as powerfully as a fire burns thousands of acres of forest.

the power of wrathful deities

Wrathful deities at first glance do not seem to symbolize enlightened Buddhas and look more like raging demons bathed in hellfire. Grasping skulls and severed heads, and trampling on corpses, they can appear quite frightening. However, when we understand that Buddhists use everything they encounter on their spiritual path, including transforming negative feelings and emotions into positive ones, we see that wrathful deities embody only the raw energy of these negativities. The imagery of wrathful deities is highly symbolic and each attribute represents one or several enlightened qualities. For example, a severed head represents cutting off attachment to the ego, thereby removing our usual dualistic thinking. The practice of tantra does not suppress negative emotions; by representing them in the form of wrathful deities the powerful energy behind destructive feelings like anger and hatred is transformed into an enlightened state, where it is used for the benefit of all beings.

In order to practice tantra, the Buddhist student must be deemed ready by his or her teacher. The student then undergoes an initiation ceremony into the practice of a particular deity by a highly qualified Tibetan lama, who can trace his lineage of oral transmission of the ceremony back to the early tantric masters of Tibet. The oral transmission is passed on to the student during the initiation, which empowers the student to do the particular tantric practice that has been given. The initiation ceremony may take several hours or days, and the student usually must make a commitment to recite daily a certain number of the deity's mantra or in some cases to recite a scripture, called a *sadhana*.

The deity resides in the center of a mandala, which is like a symbolic spiritual palace. The mandala is represented as a geometrical pattern of circles within squares within circles and has four gateways in the four directions, together with various ritual objects, minor deities, and protectors. The whole mandala is a beautiful multicolored diagram steeped in symbolism, and learning about this enhances the deity practice. Meditation on a mandala helps transform our level of consciousness because it symbolizes the transformation of experience brought about by enlightenment. The deity is pictured inside the center of the mandala but is by necessity quite small, so deities are often shown as large central figures without their mandala in the Tibetan religious paintings called *thangkas*.

Once people have been initiated into a deity practice, they develop a special relationship with that deity, known as a *yidam*, meaning personal deity. Tantric practice involves identifying oneself completely – body, speech, and mind – with one's *yidam*, who is an enlightened being. In this way, by seeing ourselves as having the enlightened qualities of the deity, our own potential for enlightenment is developed. Tantric daily ritual involves reciting the mantra of the deity, visualization meditation with the deity as the focus of attention, and visualization of oneself as the deity. Experienced tantric practitioners can hold a steady visualization of the deity within the mandala, complete with all details, for some hours, though it takes many years of meditation to achieve such concentration.

The word "tantra" means continuity, and the primary purpose of practicing tantra is familiarization. By committing to undertake a daily meditation practice, the practitioner gradually brings about the transformation of his or her consciousness into a state of enlightenment. Tantra is sometimes regarded as "the quick path," because the religious texts say that it is possible to achieve enlightenment in one

lifetime, whereas the other Buddhist paths can take eons. However, this needs to be understood in the context that only an already highly experienced Buddhist meditator is ready to take on this powerful practice of tantra. His Holiness the Dalai Lama says, "It is extremely important to have the prerequisites and all qualifications for the practice of tantra."

meditation on chenrezig

This meditation on Chenrezig helps us develop compassion. Compassion is the wish to help all beings find happiness and be free from suffering, seeking to understand the causes of suffering in order to eliminate them. This practical and realistic approach allows us to find happiness for ourselves and for others.

instructions for meditation on chenrezig

1   You will need a picture of Chenrezig, the Buddha of Compassion, to help with the visualization. This can be the seated four-armed Chenrezig, or the standing thousand-armed Chenrezig.

2   Sit comfortably in the meditation posture and after a few minutes of calm meditation reflect that compassion is the wish for all beings to be free from suffering. Make a prayer in your heart that you can overcome your negative emotions and develop love and compassion for all beings.

3   As you look at the picture of Chenrezig to remember the details, reflect that he is the living embodiment of pure unobstructed compassion, radiating love and compassion toward all beings.

Close your eyes and visualize Chenrezig as a three-dimensional figure of translucent white light. Try to feel his compassionate presence. Recite Chenrezig's mantra if you like: *Om mani padme hum*, either aloud or under your breath for as long as you like.

4   At the end of your meditation dedicate any merit from this virtuous practice for the benefit of all beings.

t'ai chi ch'uan

Although it is classed as a martial art, and associated most often with action movies, t'ai chi ch'uan is an ancient Chinese system of exercise. T'ai chi is inspired by Taoist philosophy and meditation, together with the underlying principles of the I Ching, the Book of Changes. Legends abound about the origins of t'ai chi, but the most popular of these credit Chang San-feng with creating the basic set of movements. Known as Chang San-feng the Immortal, he was an ardent student of Taoism and the I Ching.

One day he watched a crane and a snake fighting and observed how the principles of yielding and attack underlay their combat. He saw in this battle an active expression of the yin and yang principles of the I Ching, where the strong changes to the yielding, and the yielding changes to the strong. The crane and the snake resumed their fight over the following days under secret observation, and Chang San-feng gradually codified their movements into the basic form of t'ai chi ch'uan.

t'ai chi is inspired by taoist philosophy

and meditation, together with the

underlying principles of the i ching

There are several schools of t'ai chi, though the differences are subtle to the untrained observer. The most well known is the Yang School, popular in both China and the West. The Wu School developed from the Yang School and is the predominant form in Hong Kong. There are two forms, the long form and the short form, both of which are taught in the West. Serious students of t'ai chi usually learn the long form, which has 108 different postures and takes around 20 minutes to perform correctly. Most students learn the short form with 50 postures, which takes about 10 minutes. It takes approximately one year of regular classes to learn the short form and two years for the long form.

T'ai chi is a lot more complex than simple keep-fit exercises, though it is of great benefit to general health. It relaxes mind and body, helps digestion, and has a tonic effect on the heart and circulation. T'ai chi also keeps the joints mobile and flexible and, perhaps most importantly, quiets the nervous system with its slow graceful movements bringing peace and harmony. Anyone who wishes can practice t'ai chi, and groups of people practicing together are a familiar early morning sight in the parks of China and Hong Kong. A closer look often reveals that many individuals are old. Although powerful, t'ai chi is also gentle enough for people of any age to perform.

desirable qualities for practicing t'ai chi ch'uan

Just as we need to have quiet, focused awareness in order to meditate, so we need stillness and concentration to practice t'ai chi. The practitioner learns to coordinate mind, breath, and body, bringing harmony to the practice. It is said the mental attitude of the practitioner must be one of concentrated quietness so that the mind is resolute and the forms can be achieved correctly. In sitting meditation, what is outside moves inside; in t'ai chi the qualities of the inside move outside. This means if the mind is without clarity and awareness, the movements will lack quietness, energy, and harmony.

Taoists regard the breath as one of the three treasures of the body, and as we saw with mindfulness of breathing, the breath gives us our life energy. However, in t'ai chi breathing is more than just exhalation and inhalation; it also circulates our inner vital force known as chi. Sexual energy is transmuted into chi by an inner alchemical process by uniting the concentrated mind, breath, and sexual energy of a person. This is achieved by directing mental concentration and the breath into the psychic center, three inches below the navel, known as the *tan tien*. Heat, or energy, then develops and is distributed around the body as psychic energy, which then fuels the t'ai chi movements. The circulation of chi also accelerates the circulation of the blood, and together these energize the movements.

> *in sitting meditation, what is outside*
> *moves inside; in t'ai chi the qualities*
> *of the inside move outside*

This meditation and circulation of chi then produces a more subtle inner essence called spirit or *shen*, and at the most advanced level *shen* is refined to become emptiness or *shu*. Emptiness in this context means realizing the interdependent nature of the self or ego and therefore its lack of inherent existence. The t'ai chi master who has realized emptiness of self and performs the movements with total lack of ego is reputed to be indestructible. This has been demonstrated in the West on several occasions. During a t'ai chi class I witnessed the truth of this reputation as I watched a large man run at a small Chinese teacher. In a seemingly magical split second, he was sent flying with apparent ease by the t'ai chi master.

We develop the outer movements together with inner meditation and circulation of chi. All movements are performed at the same slow pace to enhance the practitioner's concentration, energy, breathing, and patience. The movements are always smooth, never sudden or abrupt. This facilitates continuity, and each movement flows seamlessly into the next with no discernible break. According to tradition, t'ai chi ch'uan has been compared to a long river that flows freely and peacefully, and this is the feeling practitioners attempt to develop. As t'ai chi practitioners repeat the sequence, whether short form or long form, they gradually develop a sense of harmonious continuity. After years of daily practice the advanced student performs the movements with the grace of a dancer. This proficiency is the ideal all students strive toward.

the correct posture for practicing t'ai chi

The practitioner must be relaxed in mind and body to perform the movements properly. When the whole body is fully relaxed, it is easier to direct the breath into the abdomen and achieve the circulation of chi. When the thighs and waist are relaxed, the whole body can move freely without tension, and relaxed legs give the body stability and lightness of movement. The upper body should be erect and centered so there is a straight line from the crown of the head to the lower abdomen. The lower body is centered by positioning the legs and feet so they can pivot easily as well as support the weight of the body. The weight is carried in the center of the feet, not in the toes or heels, to avoid fatigue. The feet are always positioned precisely to aid fluidity of movement and balance.

> *according to tradition, t'ai chi ch'uan*
> *has been compared to a long river that*
> *flows freely and peacefully*

Shifting the distribution of weight between the two feet is fundamental to t'ai chi. Sometimes all the weight is on one foot while the other is completely light, though both are firmly rooted in the ground. At other times the weight distribution is 80 to 20, or 70 to 30, but it is only ever equal at the beginning and end. The weight ratio constantly changes, promoting harmony and continuity of movement. This reflects the underlying principle of t'ai chi, which is effortlessness. Unnecessary exertion is avoided and movements are free and smooth. Less strength is more, as is seen when t'ai chi is used as self-defense, when the opponent's weight is used against him. Ideally the t'ai chi practitioner moves lightly, freely, gracefully, slowly, and without effort.

practicing t'ai chi

Several preparatory warm-up exercises are practiced before t'ai chi is performed. The one described here helps develop a fundamental principle of t'ai chi, that of shifting the weight between the feet, reflecting the movement of energy from yang into yin and back again.

instructions for t'ai chi exercise

1   Start by standing with the legs slightly apart. The knees should be slightly bent at all times during the exercise. Spend some minutes in calm meditation watching the breath, to become tranquil and focused. Move one foot forward so the two feet are diagonal. Be physically and mentally relaxed but alert. Make sure the back is straight.

2   Keeping the upper body supple, so the arms swing naturally, move all the weight onto the front foot, while ensuring that the back foot remains firmly but lightly on the ground. Aim for a light suppleness and flexibility, so the weight can easily shift back and forth.

3   Now move the weight to the back foot and repeat in a slow, graceful rhythm. Try to feel the ratio of weight as it moves between the feet, ensuring that the knees are bent at all times. Be sure not to lean over the foot that has the weight on it. Change legs after five minutes.

4   You can do this as long as you like, but your upper legs will tire after about 10 minutes if you are doing it properly but have not had much practice. When you finish, stand in calm meditation for a few minutes and reflect on the following t'ai chi saying: "The head is suspended from the heavens, and the feet are rooted in the earth."

yoga

Yoga has become enormously popular in the West during the last few decades, and every village or town hall seems to hold weekly yoga classes. It tends to be presented as a holistic fitness program that exercises and stretches every part of the body – so muscles, joints, internal organs, circulation, and respiration all benefit – while also calming the mind and emotions. All these claims are true, but there is a lot more to yoga than just a fitness program, and it is vastly more sophisticated than many of the other exercise classes offered.

Yoga is almost 3,000 years old and is an esoteric tradition of Hinduism, though it probably originated from ancient Indian shamanic practices. Yoga is a Sanskrit word meaning union, or perhaps more accurately, yoke. Yoke in this context means uniting, or literally "yoking" the lower aspect of the person, the ego personality, to the higher truth. The Bhagavad-gita, the ancient Hindu classic written in Sanskrit and meaning Lord's Song, defines yoga as balance or equanimity. Thus we can conclude that yoga is both an ultimate state of harmony with God or higher being and the method used to achieve this state of harmony.

yoga is a sanskrit word meaning union,

or perhaps more accurately, yoke

We have already looked at one of the main yoga traditions in the section on Kundalini yoga, so here we will focus on the popular perception of yoga based on hatha yoga. Hatha yoga means the forceful way, and its original aim was to transform the human body into a worthy vehicle for enlightenment. Thus yoga is not simply a set of exercises, but ultimately a way of life that attempts to realize our true nature, what is called pure being-consciousness, or attaining enlightenment. This self-realization means the realization of *atman*, the universal essence of selfhood. In this way we can see that yoga is an esoteric spiritual tradition and that what we perform in our yoga class or at home represents only a fraction of the potential of this ancient metaphysical discipline.

the origins of hatha yoga

In yoga the body is viewed as a manifestation of the divine and so the body can be used as a positive instrument for attaining liberation. Hatha yoga grew out of the siddha tradition where body cultivation – *kaya-sadhana* – was part of their path. The actual origins are obscure, but the 10th-century master Gorakshanatha is generally regarded as the first great exponent. The early hatha yoga manuals describe a wide variety of techniques for working with the life force, or prana, of the body, mainly involving pranayama, or breath control and meditative concentration. The spiritual ideal behind these practices was to achieve a strong, healthy body with the motivation to gain enlightenment, but over the years the spiritual aspiration frequently became secondary to the desire to gain the physical therapeutic benefits.

Hatha yoga teachers in the West present basic breathing techniques and periods of meditation in their classes alongside the physical exercises, which greatly benefit both mind and body. Although this simplified version of the original hatha yoga does not explore the full potential of the practice, this modern Western form more readily suits our contemporary disposition. The media tends to portray yoga as the way to health, beauty, and a slim figure, but in fact its benefits are far more wide reaching and include lengthening life and promoting a more peaceful and meaningful one. Perhaps some idea of longevity and a more spiritual approach to life may influence some aspirants, but these are generally secondary reasons for taking up yoga. However, many thousands of people benefit from this modern form and yoga, as in times past, has been adapted successfully to suit different cultural and historical conditions.

the benefits of yoga

The advantages of practicing yoga are widely recognized by many people, through either direct experience or as the result of scientific studies. It is now generally regarded as a comprehensive system for cultivating and maintaining a high level of physical fitness and mental and emotional calm. Yoga is a holistic discipline, recognizing that all systems of the body must receive attention and therefore regards body, mind, and emotions as a total entity. All the techniques work with the different aspects of the person in relation to the optimum health benefits of the whole being.

yoga is a holistic discipline, recognizing that all systems of the body must receive attention

The benefits of yoga include strengthening and revitalizing the entire body, regaining the flexibility we had when young, eliminating tension while remaining alert, and increasing endurance. The practitioner also develops balance, poise, and coordination, improves concentration, and increases resistance to many diseases. Over time the yoga practitioner also learns how to store the life force, or prana, which can then be released when needed, such as during periods of extreme stress.

The main practice in yoga are positions called asanas. The practitioner moves into the required posture and then holds it for some time with patience, concentration, and control to achieve the maximum benefit. He or she then moves on to the next asana in the sequence. Although the asanas require accurate positioning of the body, initial proficiency is unimportant. What counts is regular practice and understanding the progressive nature of the discipline. Yoga is most definitely not a competitive sport. Each practitioner progresses at his or her own pace according to his or her particular body structure, aptitude, and level of physical fitness.

It is important to incorporate the appropriate meditation while performing yoga. By bringing the single-pointed concentration of calm meditation to each asana, the effectiveness is increased by total focus on the movement or held position. This awareness of how each asana is affecting the body helps the natural progression. The basic pranayama, or breath control, in yoga works with the asanas to benefit the whole person. After some time the idea of the ego performing a set routine is transformed into the movements flowing through the whole person without the sense of someone doing it. This transformation is when yoga goes beyond just a set of physical exercises and reaches the level of spiritual practice.

by bringing the single-pointed concentration of calm meditation to each asana, the effectiveness is increased

The different asanas are performed either standing, seated, or lying. They are presented in a specific order to form a sequence that is progressive in nature and should be adhered to in order to achieve maximum benefit. Working through the asanas in the correct order also prevents pulling muscles, overstretching ligaments, or straining joints. There is a crucial difference between correctly stretching and feeling the muscles work hard to hold an asana and overdoing it and causing stress or damage to some part of the body. It is recommended to initially join a class with a respected yoga teacher to learn the basic technique before attempting to practice yoga at home by yourself. Even proficient yoga practitioners attend classes for instruction, because there is always something new to discover and there are new levels to reach in yoga.

practicing complete breath, standing

Complete Breath, Standing is often one of the first asanas in a yoga routine. It helps develop healthy, deep breathing, and breath control. This has a beneficial effect on the whole body.

instructions for complete breath, standing

I   This is a simple and basic yoga exercise that can be easily learned and practiced without any strain to the body, yet will be of benefit if practiced regularly. Stand relaxed with the feet slightly apart, in line with the shoulders, and the arms hanging loosely at the sides. Spend a few minutes in calm meditation to clear the mind and become focused.

2   Exhale slowly and completely through the nose, contracting the abdomen to ensure that there is complete exhalation with no breath left in the body. Try to experience the brief moment between exhalation and inhalation.

3   As you begin to inhale, breathe in slowly and with control. At the same time, slowly raise the arms with the palms facing upward. Expand the chest to breathe in as much air as possible.

The inhalation should finish with the arms above the head, palms touching. Be aware of the different movements of the chest as it expands to fill with air and how this is being influenced by the movement of the arms.

4   Hold the breath in this position for five seconds. Then exhale slowly, with control as you lower the arms, palms down, till the exhalation is complete and the arms are hanging relaxed at the sides. Notice the sensations at all times.

5   Repeat without pausing for five complete breaths. When you can do this comfortably and have gained some experience, you can gradually increase the number.

meditation in daily life

informal
meditation

There are many different meditation methods as we have seen, ranging from simply watching the breath to much more complex forms. However, they all share one common feature, a formal structure and methodology. This involves learning a technique and then practicing it according to a set of instructions. There is a definite beginning and an end, and afterward life continues apparently without meditation. However, if this were truly so, the different meditations would not be anywhere near as effective as they can and were designed to be. So we need to learn about informal meditation to experience its benefits in daily life.

Meditation is not simply an activity, it is a way of transforming our lives. Because our prime tool is our own mind, we are never apart from the opportunity to work with it. However, we obviously need to live our lives. We must go to work, maintain relationships with other people, prepare and eat meals, and have rest and leisure time. Even if we choose to be a monk or a nun, dedicating our lives to meditation, there are still many times when we are not in formal meditation.

perhaps the best way to describe
informal meditation is as
mindfulness in daily life

Informal meditation involves meditating between the actual meditation sessions of the various different religious traditions. This is a way of bringing the qualities of meditation into our daily lives. Meditation has been described as training the mind, and we can regard informal meditation as the practice of what we have learned and discovered in formal meditation. In this way, meditation becomes habitual and an integral part of our life.

practicing informal meditation

So how do we practice informal meditation in public situations? We obviously cannot sit cross-legged with our eyes shut. Perhaps the best way to describe informal meditation is as mindfulness in daily life. If we remain mindful as much of the time as we can, we are really living our lives. We are being present to what is happening inside ourselves, our changes of mood, and so on, and what is going on around us in our immediate environment. This helps us to make the most of our lives so that we don't run the risk of spending all our time lost in daydreams and fantasies, caught up in the unreal while missing our real life as it unfolds in the moment.

We also tend to get caught up in negative emotions, such as frustration and anger. The various spiritual traditions clearly remind us that being alive involves suffering; it is inevitable that dissatisfaction will occur because circumstances often do not go the way we would like them to. We can think about being stuck in a traffic jam that is making us late for an important appointment, for example. Normally we might become agitated, angry, and upset, and these emotions cause us suffering. However, there is another way to deal with such situations – a way in which we don't have to suffer the negative impact of anger and frustration.

being upset, angry, and
worried brings us no benefit
whatsoever; it merely aggravates
our suffering

First of all we need to remember to breathe. When we are angry or upset, our breathing changes, becoming shallow and quick, and we don't get enough oxygen into our bodies. This creates further physiological changes, creating a vicious circle. Thinking about our breathing and consciously breathing deeply will provide some level of calm. Now we need to look at the situation dispassionately. We analyze the situation and apply our reason and common sense. We understand that there is nothing we can do to change the traffic and that it is not our fault that we will be late for our appointment.

Being upset, angry, and worried brings us no benefit whatsoever; it merely aggravates our suffering. Arriving late for the appointment is inevitable, so we accept this. There is no point arriving in an emotional state, because this will not help how we behave during our appointment. Of course this sounds easy and is in fact hard to put into practice. But it is not impossible, and meditating regularly will help us remember to apply meditation in our daily life. In this way, the peace and calm developed in formal meditation are helpful in the many stressful circumstances we encounter.

meditation in nature

Meditation in nature is one of the most pleasant ways to feel alive and remember to be present to our surroundings as well as be in touch with our inner feelings. We may already do this to some extent, but it is easy to go for a walk or sit in a beautiful wood and be caught up in thoughts and fantasies, hardly noticing the trees, birds, and nature around us. This is not meditation, it is just another way of being caught up in mental activity.

We need to learn to be present to our surroundings to fully enjoy and appreciate them. Perhaps we have seen people walking deep in thought past beautiful scenery, eyes on the ground, not noticing anything around them. Such people may think they are enjoying their walk in nature, but in fact all they are noticing is their thoughts. In this way they have missed out on the whole experience of being alive, being in touch with the elements and nature.

we begin to feel a deep connection

with the life around us

We can develop a more positive attitude toward this experience and decide to be present to our experience in the woods. Before you start walking, you can stand for a few minutes and look around you. Notice everything in front of your eyes, the objects in the distance as well as close by. Really try to see. Use your sense of sight to the fullest. Bring your attention consciously to your other senses, one by one. Listen to the sounds of birds, insects, the wind through the trees. There are many little sounds we usually miss unless we consciously listen. Feel the air on your skin and how the wind moves your hair and clothes. Feel the ground beneath your feet, the softness or hardness of the earth, the crunching of twigs and leaves. Be aware of the many subtle smells around you, the scent of flowers, the moist earth, what comes on the wind.

As you start to walk, notice the new sensations through all your senses. Stop walking from time to time, and reconnect with the feeling of being present to your surroundings. When you look at the next tree, really see it. Go up and touch it, smell it, be with it. After some time of consciously being present in this natural environment, we begin to feel a deep connection with the life around us and that our life is a part of all this living happening here and now. Observe your reactions to nature, which are usually calm and peaceful, sensing the mystery of life.

Notice when your thoughts intrude on your experience. Gently let them go, and reaffirm your decision to be in nature fully. If you lose the sense of interconnectedness, stand still for a while and spend some minutes watching your breath, observing how your thoughts arise and pass. Find a place to sit and try turning toward the sun and shutting your eyes. Feel the sun's warmth and light and be aware of how it helps life to exist. Shutting your eyes allows the other senses to become more sensitive, so you can explore these sensations in more depth.

Once you have become calm and quiet, and thoughts are not racing through your mind, be present to your inner silence. Somehow we have become full of nature, and we realize that we are not apart from it, but a part of it. Perhaps the sense of an ego self recedes, and it is not you who is experiencing being in nature; there is simply being. Rest in this space for as long as you can. When you return to the hurly-burly of daily life, you can recall these tranquil moments in nature. Visualize the trees and flowers that you noticed, recollect the calm and peace, and resolve to create space in your life to be in nature as often as you can.

eating

When we incorporate meditation into our lives, we naturally become more sensitive and aware, particularly about our lifestyle and health. Perhaps we see meditation as being part of a religion or spiritual tradition. We may wish to embrace that religion's ethical guidelines for living a responsible life, to find true happiness. Most spiritual traditions encourage a moderate or "middle way" approach to the body and the senses. This means we neither overindulge in sensory experiences such as eating or drinking too much nor damage our bodies by depriving them of necessary food. We can regard our body as the temple of the soul or spirit, and in the same way as we would maintain a temple building, we look after our body by providing adequate nourishment.

In our Western culture we have left the middle way and moved to over-consumption and accumulation of consumer goods. This has contributed to the proliferation of eating disorders, such as obesity, anorexia, and bulimia, which have tragically increased alongside material affluence. Eating too much, or too little, or obsessively indicates an unhealthy attitude toward life and the body in

particular, and often the lack or neglect of spiritual values. Though obviously someone with an eating disorder should seek professional help, we can all reflect upon this malaise and find our own middle way in our eating habits.

Another unfortunate consequence of our contemporary urban lifestyle is the proliferation of fast food. By eating too much of this relatively unhealthy food option, we are not respecting our bodies because we are not providing them with sufficient nutrition. Burgers, chips, and other fried foods often lack basic nutrients and contain too much fat, salt, chemical additives, and sugars. In addition to being unhealthy, these substances can aggravate allergies and in some instances are linked with eating disorders. The whole notion of fast food is built around eating quickly, often on the run. This is also unhealthy. To obtain the optimum nutrition from food, we need to eat slowly and chew well, preferably sitting down so we can digest our food properly.

eating as a form of meditation

To counter unhealthy and unsatisfactory ways of eating, we can think of eating properly as a form of meditation, eating meditation. We need to choose food that is nutritious, that benefits and does not harm the body. Fresh fruit, vegetables, and whole grains make a good basis. We need to eat sufficient protein, though scientific studies have shown that Western adults tend to eat more protein than they need. However, we must not obsess about eating, so the middle way approach is best, where we try to eat healthfully as often as we can.

We need to consider how our food is produced. Some people choose to be vegetarian in order to minimize the suffering and death of animals. Some choose organic food out of respect for the environment and their bodies. By contemplating where our food comes from, we can each decide what foodstuffs we wish to eat. The tradition of saying grace before meals has largely gone out of fashion, but we can spend a few moments before we start eating, to reflect on the many animals and people involved in producing our meal, and mentally thank them.

Finally we need to consider how we eat. As with all meditations, the essence is mindful awareness, so we try to be mindful of how we are eating our food as well as the foods we have selected. Try eating with mindful awareness. Bring the food slowly toward your mouth, chew each mouthful with awareness of what you are doing, and notice all the different textures, flavors, and so on. When we eat with mindfulness, we can actually enjoy the process at an entirely new level. Be mindful of the food as you swallow and bring your attention to your body's digestive processes after the meal. By eating with mindful awareness, we reinforce the other meditations we practice and this helps us live our lives fully and well.

waking up
and going to sleep

We usually have a few conscious moments in bed before falling asleep and, if we make the time, we can also have some moments of reflection before we get up and start our day. These are precious moments for recollection of our activities during the day or of our dreams during the night. These moments are also precious because they are often peaceful, quiet, and relaxed, and we have the opportunity to be with ourselves as we truly are, before we become a mother, a teacher, a scientist, or whatever role we play during the day.

The times before going to sleep and waking up exist on the threshold of changing levels of consciousness. We often describe this as drifting into sleep or slowly waking up as our consciousness moves through subtle changes. If we can maintain awareness of what we are experiencing, we can learn something about how our mind works. What actually happens to our mind and consciousness between being awake and asleep is amazing, though we usually take it for granted because we are so familiar with the process.

what actually happens to our mind

and consciousness between being

awake and asleep is amazing

Time spent on the borderline between wakefulness and sleep is therefore an interesting time to practice informal meditation. Before going to sleep, we can review the events of the day. Even if nothing remarkable happened, we can reflect on the range of emotions and feelings we experienced while interacting with others and participating in different activities. Perhaps one troublesome event will stick in our mind, its intensity submerging everything else, making it difficult to go to sleep. Whatever our experience, we now have the opportunity to see things in perspective and let go of any negative feelings.

regarding each day as if it were the last

Going to sleep is sometimes called a *petit mort* or little death, because we lose consciousness, albeit temporarily. We can use this notion to reflect on the fact that each day is precious and could be our last. Our recollections of the day may seem mundane at first glance, but if we regard each day as if it were our last, we find it has more value. If, on the other hand, we are stuck with one troublesome event, such as an argument with our partner or poor treatment by our boss, we can use this time to see these experiences in perspective. If we think of our whole life and the immensity of what happens throughout its course, we can see that though we are currently troubled by this one event, it is probably a relatively minor occurrence that we will forget within a week or so. Regarding the situation like this lessens its emotional impact and allows us to go to sleep peacefully.

Our awakening each day is like a rebirth into new consciousness from out of the dream world. It is a shame to waste these precious moments by having to leap up and start our day immediately. It may feel like a sacrifice, but if we set the alarm clock for 10 minutes earlier, we gain the luxury of time to recollect our dreams or prepare ourselves for the day ahead. This does require discipline; otherwise, our attachment to sleep will send us back to the land of nod. If we can awaken with the motivation to recollect our dreams, even writing them down, then we can use this time beneficially.

because dreams exist in another level
of consciousness, we tend to
forget them soon after waking

Dreams are the unconscious trying to bring issues through to waking consciousness, and we can learn a lot from them if we are so inclined. Because dreams exist in another level of consciousness, we tend to forget them soon after waking, so writing them down immediately can help us remember them. We can spend the 10 minutes reflecting on our dreams to see if there is anything that feels important and work out what our unconscious might be trying to tell us. The surreal language of dreams is not always obvious, but we can learn to interpret them with practice. If we learn how to interpret our dream language we will discover a narrative gradually emerging from the apparently random chaos of images. Dreams are deeply personal and we need to use our own analysis rather than just relying on the classic interpretation of images in dream dictionaries. Noting recurrent symbols and patterns will help us discover what our unconscious psychological life is trying to tell us. We can then practice insight meditation on the recurrent themes and archetypal images. This will help us move toward an integrated understanding of our dream life and its relevance to waking consciousness and daily life.

cleaning, driving, and other activities

The idea of actually enjoying washing the dishes, doing the laundry, or managing other mundane chores probably seems an impossibility for most people. But imagine what life might look like if we embraced them instead of avoiding them. Rather than secretly wishing them away, what if we approached them with an open mind and the realization that they too could speak to us and reveal something meaningful about ourselves and the world around us?

We all know that much of life is spent doing repetitive, mundane tasks that we may find boring, irritating, or frustrating. We don't look forward to washing the dishes after dinner, cleaning the house, and mowing the lawn. Even our basic hygiene requirements may seem tedious at times and if we are very tired, the last thing we want to do is shower or do the laundry. If we add up all the time we spend doing such basic chores, we find little time left over for the activities that give us pleasure. So the question arises of how we can make these everyday activities less boring and more enjoyable. We might think there is something intrinsically boring about our routine activities, that if we took away the necessity of having to do them our lives would improve and become more interesting or exciting. But consider the number of labor-saving devices that have come into our lives over the last few decades. Despite the promise of these gadgets to give us more leisure time and more happiness, we discover that we have filled our time up with other activities that don't bring us real happiness in the way we thought they would. Sometimes they even become tedious and not so different from our household chores.

renunciation doesn't mean we have

to give up the things we enjoy

or that enjoyment is wrong in any way

If we have a demanding job with long hours, we may employ a cleaner for our house, someone to do our laundry, wash our car, and so on. However, we then find ourselves in a vicious circle: we need to work extra hours or take the more demanding, higher-paid job just to keep paying others to do the mundane chores in our life. Eventually, late one night, still stressed out from our job, we arrive home

to our immaculately cleaned house only to realize we have not found the happiness we had hoped for by removing the mundane from our life.

It is part of human nature to experience dissatisfaction, and the best approach is to simply accept it. Buddhists use the principle of renunciation to help accept the prevalence of dissatisfaction. Renunciation doesn't mean we have to give up the things we enjoy or that enjoyment is wrong in any way. It means renouncing or consciously giving up our attachment to the activities and possessions we enjoy, so that when they are replaced with things and activities we don't find so pleasurable, such as daily chores, we don't experience suffering from losing what is enjoyable. Renunciation also means accepting what we don't like without fighting against it or trying to avoid it, realizing that the things we don't like are inevitable but will in turn be replaced by something else.

learning to enjoy our activities

The truth is that there is nothing in cleaning, driving, or tidying that is inherently unsatisfactory. It is our reaction to how we undertake these activities that creates our feelings of boredom or irritation. Since we cannot change the fact that we have to drive to work five days a week through rush-hour traffic, we can at least change our reactions and feelings instead. This then becomes an informal meditation on how to transform our approach to mundane activities, and learning how to accept and even enjoy them.

There is an old saying that there is no way to happiness, because happiness itself is the way. Such a reminder is useful when approaching chores. Usually we think, "Oh no, cleaning the house is going to be so boring and unpleasant. I'll do it quickly to get it out of the way and do something enjoyable afterward." If instead we decide to make the most of this activity by changing our attitude, we may be pleasantly surprised. As the saying reminds us, we can find happiness only in how we live our life moment to moment. We don't find happiness by wishing that we were somewhere else, doing something else instead.

First we need to accept unconditionally that we are about to clean the house, rather than finding a way to avoid it or resenting it. Then instead of feeling resigned, which makes us dull and sullen, we make the decision to investigate what it actually feels like to clean without all our preconceived ideas about it – for example, that it's boring, beneath us, or anything else. We try to approach cleaning the house as if we were doing it for the first time and pay attention to all the little details we normally rush through or ignore.

dish-washing meditation

In cleaning meditation our attention is on the cleaning. We avoid escaping into our thoughts and fantasies or listening to the radio and remain in the present. Dish-washing meditation transforms a routine chore into another experience. We can start by resolving to wash the dishes without the usual resignation and thoughts that it is boring. Slowly gather up the different dishes, pans, cutlery, and glasses. As you pick up each item, notice it; observe the pattern, color, and shape. Try not to make judgments on fleeting thoughts you may have as you look at each item. Simply let them arise and pass. Enjoy the details, the simple actions involved, and what you're accomplishing by cleaning each item. You may surprise yourself and discover you are enjoying this new way of washing dishes. You may even eventually become more thoughtful about how to spend your time and make conscious decisions to change certain aspects of your life. Realizing that the simple things in life have more to offer than you originally thought, you will see that rushing through your chores is not the path to happiness. Bringing the meditative mind to all mundane tasks will help you enjoy life more because you will be living each moment, rather than wishing you were somewhere else instead.

instructions for dish-washing meditation

I   Pile the items carefully, mindfully on the counter rather than just mindlessly heaping them in a jumble. You can try treating each object as if it were a valuable antique or reflect on how someone living in poverty, who has only one plate, would treat it. Don't take the dishes for granted just because you can. As you run the hot water, reflect how lucky you are to be able to do this, how this simple act would be an unheard of luxury for many people around the world. Try not to waste the precious resource of water and run only the amount you need. As you mindfully add the soap and agitate the water to make it frothy, simply be present to the experience. Look at the bubbles, how they reflect the light, how the water feels running over your hands.

2   Mindfully wash the dishes. Be present to each item, wash it carefully, and place it to dry. Don't judge the experience or try to rush through it; just think that this is what you are doing at this time. Reflect that if you spent all your dish-washing moments wishing you were doing something else instead, you would be wishing away a lot of your life. Life is uncertain and can be short, so if boredom starts to creep in to your experience, reflect on how you would feel if this were one of the last activities you would ever do.

3   Try to be present to the whole experience. Look for details of dish washing that you may have missed previously in the rush to finish and try to reevaluate your feelings about the task at hand. Don't just take it for granted that you dislike this mundane task. We can practice meditation like this throughout our daily life in the many activities we do, remembering to be present to and mindful of whatever we are doing. We may find we can enjoy some of these activities or that we have discovered something new about them, or at least reduced our dislike of them.

relaxation
and vacations

These are the precious moments we have been looking forward to. All day we think about what we will do in our free time after work. All year we wait enthusiastically for our annual vacation. Finally these eagerly anticipated moments of rest and vacation arrive. We watch television, play sports, go out for a drink with our friends, sightsee, shop, and so on. These are fun, we enjoy them, and they help us make the necessary separation from being at work. However, they are all activities. They are doing rather than being. If we spend some of our leisure time simply being, we can enter a new dimension that will make us feel healthier, happier, more relaxed, and thoroughly rested.

going on vacation

Let's look at our annual vacation. We make endless preparations, some of which are essential but many of which are not. We go shopping with the idea that we "need" lots of new clothes, cosmetics, and so forth, and spend a lot of our hard-earned money. We go through the arduous journey to our destination and finally arrive. We study maps and guidebooks and set ourselves a sightseeing agenda where we cram in as much as possible so we will have seen everything and photographed it all. We eat and drink too much to compensate for having dieted to look good for our vacation. We arrive home exhausted. We tell everyone what a great time we had and doubtless we have some great memories, but perhaps we notice that we are as tired as when we went away, if not more so. We then start looking forward to our next vacation because we need a rest!

We think this is how we should spend our vacation because this is what everyone else does, and when we are at our vacation location we are encouraged to consume and spend as much money as possible. However, by making some space in our fearsome sightseeing agenda, and resisting the temptation to "shop till we drop," we can have some time to really rest. The British word for vacation is holiday, which is derived from "holy day," days originally spent quietly resting from work and contemplating God or the meaning of life, or performing other religious practices. So we can include some time for holiday meditation in the spirit of the original holy days.

Of course we want to have fun and see new places, too, but there is no point in doing and seeing everything just because it is there. If we consider carefully the choices open to us, we can select what we really want to do. We may enjoy our excursions more if there are fewer of them because we can spend longer at each place. Instead of rushing on to the next location, we can spend time looking carefully at all the details, smelling and hearing the unique smells and sounds. We can sit quietly and soak up the atmosphere, discovering for ourselves the qualities of the place, rather than reading about them in the guidebook.

Often we travel to hot places, where it is traditional to take a siesta. We, too, can take siestas. Sitting quietly on a balcony or under a large shady tree, we can watch the world go by and notice the infinite little details that make each culture unique. This is time for being rather than doing, so we practice simply being, feeling what it is like to be alive from moment to moment. We can also do this while walking along the beach, in the forest, or inside an ancient castle. We can try being silent some of the time and talk later rather than have chatter disrupt our experience. In this way we return from "being" on vacation, rested and refreshed.

in the workplace

The workplace might seem like an odd place to practice informal meditation; we are, after all, supposed to be working. But consider how much time we spend at work. It forms a large part of our lives, especially if we include the time spent preparing for and traveling to and from our workplace. If we do not like our job very much and feel we are doing it only to earn a living, we must explore ways to make the most of it or sacrifice much of our life to feelings of negativity. Our attitude and relationship to our work matter as much as the responsibilities of our job, and though we can't radically change our job, we can transform our negative disposition toward it.

our attitude and relationship to
our work matter as much as the
responsibilities of our job

Just hearing the simple word "work" can send us into a spiral of resistance, stress, and anxiety. We immediately start worrying about how much work we have and our competence to carry out our tasks effectively, or we enter a mind state of impotent hatred about our job. Perhaps we are unemployed and desperately seeking a job, in which case we crave work and become jealous of those who have jobs. One easy way to help transform our attitude toward work is to consider the alternative. If we are employed we can think about those who don't have a job and the impact of joblessness on self-worth and survival. Likewise, if we are unemployed, we consider the long hours, stress, and routine boredom of those with jobs. In this way, we can experience the positive aspects of both employment and unemployment.

Even if we are lucky and have a job we enjoy that pays well, or are rich and can choose unemployment without suffering financial deprivation, work, or the lack of it, can still have negative connotations. Imagine your ideal job, perhaps something glamorous like being an actress, artist, or musician. Then reflect on the insecure nature of such work, the potential for creative despair, the long unsociable hours. This brings the realization that all forms of work have a downside to them; there is no perfect job. Perhaps we envy those few rich people who don't have to work and have lives of luxury, but many of them are not happier, only richer and more comfortable. These people often experience a sense of worthlessness, although this may be unconscious and manifest itself in self-destructive ways. Without some meaningful activity, even if this is just earning our living, life can seem empty and worthless.

dealing with office politics

Most of us work with other people, colleagues and bosses. In light of the numerous hours spent at work, such relationships are important because they form such a large part of our lives. But in the same way we can choose our friends but not our family, we also cannot choose our work colleagues. We may have to spend long periods of time cooperating with people whom we find it difficult to get along with (inevitably conflict will arise), and it is notoriously difficult to remain diplomatic all the time with the many different issues of office politics. For example, you may have a difficult boss, a person who habitually becomes angry when work problems arise. This affects not only you, but all your colleagues as well, so there is a collective responsibility for dealing with the boss's inappropriate anger. You can try discussing different ways to deal with this with your colleagues, and agree to tackle the issue as a group. If this seems too difficult or ambitious, then try discussing the problem with friends and family outside work, and try to find an objective solution. Most importantly, when confronted by an angry boss or work colleague, remember to breathe deeply. You do not have to react either by becoming intimidated or angry yourself. Try to keep focused on the issue and quietly suggest ways to deal with it.

by…maintaining a friendly attitude
toward our colleagues, we can…improve
the workplace for everyone

It is useful to reflect on how we relate to others at work. If we don't get along with colleagues, we can try to find ways to improve these relationships. In the same way that there may be no ideal job, there may also be no ideal workmate. But by actively maintaining a friendly attitude toward our colleagues, we can perhaps transform unpleasant situations and improve the workplace for everyone. We can still work side by side with people who have different views from us by simply avoiding potentially difficult subjects. This may even mean our conversations are somewhat superficial, but by being friendly and skillful in how we relate to colleagues, we help create a good working atmosphere. Bringing meditative reflection and mindfulness into our work situation can help us change our attitudes and actions, transforming the whole experience into something more pleasant for everyone.

conflict resolution

Conflict is an inevitable part of life. It is a challenge we can live up to and respond appropriately to, learning something and moving on with more wisdom. Or we can remain stuck in the same old patterns and ways of responding and not grow or move on. Conflict is neither inherently good nor bad; it is how we respond that matters. Learning how to resolve conflict skillfully is important, a life skill that will serve us well time and again. An important first step is to recognize the inevitability of conflict in daily life and realize its positive potential. In doing so, we can learn how to work with conflict in constructive ways.

We can ask ourselves, "How do I respond to conflict?" To answer this question in depth we need to return to our childhood to see the first lessons we had in dealing with conflict. The adults around us, especially our parents, will have dealt with conflict in particular ways that will have made a lasting impression upon us. Perhaps our mother shouted angrily or became quiet and sullen, or our father refused to listen and deal with problems. We will have learned our childhood responses to conflict (largely unconsciously) from how our parents reacted, sometimes from fear or misunderstanding. It is useful to spend some time recollecting early memories about situations of conflict in order to understand your childhood feelings about it.

conflict is neither inherently good nor bad; it is how we respond that matters. ...learning how to resolve conflict skillfully is important

We can then ask ourselves how we deal with conflict as an adult, remembering that we have inherited some of the ways we respond to conflict. Be honest with yourself. It is all too easy to have an idealized vision of ourselves or to see ourselves as worse than we are. Do you respond by being quiet or confrontational? Do you enjoy arguing with others or hate conflict? Once we have assessed how we deal with conflict, we can contemplate the fact that this behavior is not set in stone. We can relearn our responses to conflict. If you decide that you do not deal with conflict well, you can take comfort from the fact that you can change these unsatisfactory responses if you want to.

There is no point in trying to wish conflict away, and there is a high price to pay for suppressing conflict, either from fear of engaging with others or from misguided ideas of politeness and good manners. Conflict can be constructive, and when dealing with conflict we can learn a lot about ourselves and others. Conflict is a way of getting to know each other better, because the veneer of polite, socially acceptable behavior is stripped off to reveal who we really are. Of course this makes us vulnerable and often this is a major reason we are afraid to engage in conflict. However, if we have the courage to meet others positively and honestly in conflict situations, we have the potential to find personal freedom far beyond our negative and fearful responses to conflict.

Fear makes us behave differently; it alters our normal behavior, so we need to meet our fears openly and look at ways of transforming them. One of the most powerful methods of fear transformation is undertakig active listening exercises with other people. Hearing each other's life stories helps humanize our response to the other, whom we may have unconsciously demonized in our mind. If we don't know the myriad little details of someone's life – their childhood, family, feelings, work experiences, and relationships – then it is easy not to see them as human and fragile, just like ourselves. They remain the mysterious and demon-like "other" with whom we have no real relationship. By listening to someone's life story, we find out who that person really is and discover our many similarities. By discovering our common human experiences, we relate much more easily and authentically to others.

> *conflict is a way of getting to know each*
> *other better, because the veneer of polite,*
> *socially acceptable behavior is stripped*
> *off to reveal who we really are*

active listening

Active listening can be a simple way to get to know someone better or an important and powerful tool in transforming conflict. Next time you find yourself in a conflict situation, take courage in both hands and suggest sitting down and discussing ways to resolve the problem. This can be done either there and then or later, when feelings have cooled down. If there are more than two of you, suggest that the group split into pairs. Start by sitting together in silence, each person watching his or her breath and connecting with his or her feelings, including the deep ones beyond the immediate superficial feelings of anger and frustration.

Take 5 to 10 minutes for this or however long people feel they need. Then suggest another couple of minutes of silent sitting during which everyone reflects upon the phrase "When I am heard I feel respected."

Then commence the active listening exercise. This involves one person speaking and the other person listening for a timed period, then trading roles. No interruptions are allowed. The listener will have a turn to speak when the first person has finished. The speaker begins by expressing the causes and the background to his or her feelings and why he or she feels troubled, but must make sure not to apportion blame to anyone for the conflict. The listener pays full careful attention to the content of what is being said and also tries to hear the underlying feelings. Conflict involves many different feelings, not just anger. Frustration, sadness, fear, loneliness, and other feelings are all present in conflict situations. When the time is up, the listener then reflects back to the speaker what he or she has heard, summarizing

what was said and the feelings expressed. The speaker responds by saying how accurate this was and reiterating any feelings or points that were missed. Then speaker and listener change roles.

we are all participants in the process of conflict, and it is possible that we have unconsciously contributed to the situation and need to take responsibility for it

Exercises such as this active listening one help us learn to respect each other's differences. All people involved in a conflict situation feel like a victim to some extent, and we need to acknowledge this to each other. If we feel we have been offended, perhaps we have also given offense. This could be active, by saying or doing something someone else found offensive, but it could just as well be passive, by not doing or saying something that the other person felt was required.

We need to be honest about our passivity. It is all too easy not to intervene when things are difficult, but if our avoidance of conflict causes things to get worse, then we must take responsibility for our inaction. We are all participants in the process of conflict, and it is possible that we have unconsciously contributed to the situation and need to take responsibility for it. However, responsibility is not blame and the difference between them needs to be clear.

Everyone involved probably agrees that change is needed in order to prevent unnecessary conflict from arising again. We might feel that the other person or people need to change first before we will make a change ourselves, but this is unhelpful. Conflict can be part of a cycle, but we can change this by choosing not to wait for the other person or people to change first and by being willing to take the first steps. We can celebrate each individual and his or her point of view as an essential part of the community, whether this is at work, at home, or in some social group.

Everyone feels the need to belong to a group and, although this is perfectly normal and healthy, we need to be careful to express belonging creatively in ways that do not cause others to feel like outsiders. If our group relies on "us and them" characterizations, we have fallen into distorted negative ways of expressing our identity and belonging. We then need to find positive ways to express our identity that are not against the other. This helps prevent superfluous conflict, and when conflict does arise, we can use it positively and creatively to learn something and move forward in life.

devotional practice and ritual

creating
a sacred space

The archetypal sacred space, or *temenos*, is often described as a place between the different worlds where the divine and the earthly meet. The concept of sacred space refers to both a physical space outside ourselves and to our own personal inner space. When we meditate, we create an inner sacred space that is receptive to divine influence and spiritual inspiration. If we meditate inside or in close proximity to a physical sacred space, the power of our meditation is strengthened by the spiritual atmosphere contained within this outer sacred space.

the concept of sacred space refers to both

a physical space outside ourselves and

to our own personal inner space

We can feel the power of sacred places when we visit religious buildings. As we enter through the doorway, a boundary separating the mundane space from the sacred, we feel the subtle change of atmosphere. A feeling of reverence naturally starts to arise within us, whether or not we have a connection with the particular religious tradition of the church, cathedral, mosque, synagogue, or temple. Because these sacred spaces have been used, often for centuries, for prayer, meditation, and devotional practices, they have become suffused with the spiritual fervor and the meditative silence of the many thousands of devotees who have prayed within these hallowed environments. We thereby connect with this atmosphere of accumulated spirituality when we cross the threshold. Meditating and praying are strengthened when practiced in these places.

Sacred places of worship are not exclusively buildings. Natural places of power exist in nature, which have also been used for spiritual practice. During a walk we may stumble across a glade in a wood, a natural circle of trees, or a curve by the river that makes us want to stop and spend time there because it has a special atmosphere. Some of these places will have been used for one form or another of religious practice. In such sacred places the natural powers of the universe join with the accumulation of prayer, ritual, and meditation that have taken place over the centuries. This creates sacred spaces that unite human religious endeavor, natural energies, and divine inspiration.

There are many sacred mountains around the world, including Uluru (or Ayers Rock) in Australia, which is sacred to Aborigines, Mount Sinai in Israel, which is sacred to Jews, and Mount Kailash in Tibet, which is sacred to Buddhists and Hindus. These sacred mountains are legendary in each respective religion as places of spiritual power and sanctuary. The arduous climb to reach the pinnacle of a mountain reflects the spiritual struggle humans experience as they attempt to ascend toward God or another divine being.

in the early religions and in magic ritual
often a simple but clearly delineated circle
was sufficient to create the sacred space

Other natural places of power include sites such as Glastonbury and Avebury in southwest England, which are located at the confluence of ley lines. Ley lines can be described as the earth's meridians, lines of natural energy that intensify when they conjoin. There are many stone circles like Avebury throughout the British Isles and Ireland, but perhaps the most famous is Stonehenge. The sheer size of the stones and the enormous task of bringing them together show the great importance of natural sacred spaces for spiritual practice in past times. However, the energies in these sacred spaces are not always entirely peaceful; sacrifice – both human and animal – sometimes formed a part of ancient spiritual practice.

The different religions each use their own distinctive iconography in creating sacred spaces, although they all share certain features. For example, sacred spaces need to be enclosed within clearly defined boundaries in order to contain the energies, or spiritual power, that accumulates there through years of worship. In the early religions and in magic ritual a simple but clearly delineated circle was often sufficient to create the sacred space. Circles are infinite, with no discernible beginning or end on the circumference. This represents the idea of the earthly and the divine flowing together in the endless dance of creation.

the tibetan mandala

One of the most fascinating sacred spaces is the Tibetan Buddhist mandala. The practice of meditating on a mandala unites both microcosm, the inner sacred space of the meditator, and macrocosm, the outer sacred space of the mandala. In this way everything becomes sacred space; there is no discrimination between inner and outer. A mandala is an iconographical representation of both the Buddhist cosmos and the human being. Just as the mandala is created around a central deity, called a *yidam*, so the human being is created around the heart center, where the mystery of ultimate spiritual reality lies.

Mandalas are intricate concentric designs, symbolizing the majestic palace in which the central deity resides, like a spiritual house. They are either painted or constructed out of colored sand in a ceremony that can last for many days. They incorporate the Buddhist teaching of impermanence, because once their ritual purpose is finished, the sand is swept up and ceremoniously thrown into the nearest source of running water. Every sand mandala is made following strict and intricate ceremonial rules, ensuring that its sacred nature is created authentically. The mandala is a deeply sacred object. Buddhists believe that just seeing it is healing for the ordinary spectator, whereas for those who are initiated into its esoteric practices, viewing the mandala subliminally triggers their powers of visualization. Those who view a mandala with goodwill and faith and feel moved by its presence will strengthen their impulse toward reaching enlightenment.

A mandala is a model for contemplative visualization practice by the initiate. Once the meditator has received the relevant initiation by a qualified tantric master, he or she develops the ability to see him- or herself as being present within the perfected environment of the mandala. Visualizing the sacred space as being composed of radiant jewel-like light through single-pointed concentration and inner vision, the meditator rests secure from mundane disturbances. In the same way that Mahayana Buddhists strive for enlightenment not for their own peace but for the benefit of all sentient beings, so residing in the bliss of the mandala is only a prerequisite for further development of this esoteric practice.

By symbolically entering the mandala through concentration and visualization, the meditator is literally practicing what the enlightened state feels like by resting in the purified sacred space. This dimension of sacred space is then internalized when the meditator starts to relate his or her inner subtle nervous system of psychic channels to the perfected outer world of the mandala. So through creative imagination and guided visualization the meditator unites both inner and outer sacred spaces on the journey to enlightenment.

Although we clearly have the physical outer sacred spaces of churches and temples, stone circles and mountains, and the inner sacred space of the spiritual aspirant, the ultimate purpose is to move beyond this duality into a unified sacred space. Neither specifically inner nor outer, the sacred space becomes all-pervasive and acts to transform mundane reality into a perfected state of being. Each time we prepare ourselves for meditation and commence our practice we have the potential to access this perfected sacred space. In this way we transform our mundane selves and mundane world into the fully enlightened state.

creating an altar

Creating an altar is part of an ages-old devotional tradition in many of the world's religions. It is not essential to create a personal altar, and your meditation will not be adversely affected if you decide not to. However, if this devotional aspect of religious practice appeals to you, then creating an altar can help make the place you meditate in feel more spiritual and enrich your practice of meditation.

Once you have created an altar for the purpose of doing meditation and other spiritual practice, it becomes a sacred space, a dedicated place for offering both physical offerings and inner offerings of prayer. Your altar is a personal creation and forms part of your devotional expression to whichever higher spiritual being you feel affinity with. Your altar, and all the offerings you place on it collectively, act as a conduit between the spiritual and mundane worlds. In this way creating an altar facilitates reverence and the inclination for meditation and prayer.

your altar, and all the offerings you place

on it collectively, act as a conduit between

the spiritual and mundane worlds

Place on your altar whatever offerings you feel are appropriate. If you are Christian, these will include symbols of the cross, Jesus, Mary, and so on; if you are Buddhist, you will include statues and pictures of the different Buddhas and bodhisattvas, and so on for each religion. If you feel no empathy with any one spiritual tradition but have a more general interest, then you are free to create a nondenominational altar with images from any religion you wish to include. What is important is that the symbols you choose have spiritual meaning for you. There is not much point in trying to include images that do not resonate with your inner being just because you feel you ought to include them or because you think they look nice.

The best place to create an altar is obviously where you meditate, which ideally is a quiet and private room, a personal sanctuary from daily life activities. A low table, shelf, or mantelpiece are all suitable for a simple altar. Simplicity is of the essence. Just as in music the different notes are given meaning by the intervals, the spaces between your offerings are important to the overall effect of the altar. You might went to cover your altar with a beautiful cloth before placing your offerings on it. The altar should be situated so you can sit in front of it. Whether you sit on a chair or a cushion on the floor does not matter. Sitting quietly looking at and contemplating the devotional symbols on your altar increases the aptitude for meditation and can deepen your understanding of whichever religion or spiritual philosophy you are practicing.

Carefully choose the major icon or icons you wish to place on your altar. Quality is better than quantity, and a simple, uncluttered altar is more conducive to meditation than a crowd of objects jostling for attention. One large beautiful statue or picture can be sufficient of Jesus, Mary, Isis, Allah, Buddha, Kali, Shiva, or whichever deity you feel closest to. If you prefer, the central object can be a crystal, stone, or nature symbol. Whatever symbolizes spiritual wisdom for you is what matters. You can regard this central figure as a primary meditation object and by using analysis, single-pointed concentration, and visualization meditations your mind and the icon will eventually become inseparable. Eventually you will be able to see it clearly in your mind whenever you wish.

offerings to the divine

Everything you place on your altar becomes an offering to the divine and to your own inner potential for enlightenment. Devotion goes beyond the idea of a humble devotee offering appeasement to an external god "up there." A deeper level of devotion is about realizing the power of Jesus working through you or cultivating your own innate Buddhahood. The nature of our offerings needs to reflect the fact that we are making them to our highest spiritual ideal. We offer only what is pure, fresh, and beautiful – the very best things we can. Traditional offerings include lighted candles, a bowl or several of fresh water, some flowers, and incense. However, you can offer whatever you feel is beautiful and gratifying to the senses. It is respectful to keep your altar clean and to make offerings daily or at least as a preparation for each time you meditate.

traditional offerings include lighted
candles, a bowl or several of fresh water,
some flowers, and incense

Lighting candles is an offering of heat and light and may have originated from worship of the sun. Flames are also purifying, and the flickering, insubstantial nature of a lighted candle is a symbol of impermanence. We can reflect upon our own mortality, our fragile life, as we observe the candle slowly burning down until it eventually dies out. Water is a powerful purification symbol and in addition to offering water on an altar, certain religions require followers to wash the hands, mouth, or feet. Even today in modern industrial Tokyo, you can stumble across an

old Shinto shrine sandwiched between modern tower blocks. Just inside the entrance is an ornate trough of water with several wooden spoons suspended above for the purpose of ritual washing before undertaking spiritual practice. Placing one or more small bowls of water upon your altar is a traditional offering of purity.

We also offer a small vase of flowers. Flowers make lovely offerings. Their fragility in lasting only a few days reminds us of impermanence, and their scent and beauty are pleasing to the senses. So although we are making offerings to a higher spiritual being or power and to our potential for enlightenment, we also enjoy the scent and beauty of these offerings as we meditate. In some small way our altar is heavenly or like a pure land, and by recreating a symbol of this here on earth we help ourselves to eventually attain such a spiritual state.

incense and other offerings

The smoke of incense was traditionally used to drive away evil spirits as well as provide an offering of sweet scent ascending to please the gods. Frankincense is a traditional ingredient of incense, used in both Eastern religions and Catholicism. Modern science reveals that frankincense has a tonic effect on the respiratory system by slowing down our breathing. This helps produce a meditative state. So by burning frankincense we make offerings to our god or higher being and at the same time increase our propensity for meditation.

You can also place objects from nature on your altar that reflect the different seasons and the passing of time, such as a budding spring twig or a red autumn leaf. Conversely, a stone from a riverbed, washed smooth by running water over many years, can remind us of the enduring quality of nature in relation to our own brief time on earth. Anything you wish to be blessed can be placed on or in front of the altar before a meditation session, and you can imagine the sacred space of the altar subtly influencing the object. If you follow one religious tradition exclusively, it is best to be guided by what that tradition suggests in terms of offerings. Otherwise you can offer whatever feels appropriate at any given time.

If you decide to create an altar, it is a good idea to make the commitment to renew the offerings daily as a sign of respect to your higher spiritual authority. When you make your daily offerings, you may also wish to genuflect or do prostrations. In the same way that we make offerings to both our spiritual guide and our own inner spiritual potential, genuflecting or prostrating ourselves honors both. In this way we are not "bowing down to graven images" or abasing ourselves, though obviously humility is part of all devotional practice. We can use the time we spend making offerings to reflect upon our motivation for practicing meditation and in this way remain clear about why we meditate.

christian prayer
in everyday life

Bringing prayer into everyday life brings us closer to God. Prayer need not be confined to the church pew or kneeling by the side of our bed last thing at night. We can pray to God in daily life situations for inspiration and strength. We can turn to God in silent prayer to help us find inner peace and patience at any time; he will always hear us. Because God listens to our thoughts as much as our speech, silent prayer is as powerful and effective as spoken prayer. God is aware of the motivation behind our prayers, and not drawing attention to ourselves by giving outward signs of prayer can be the most skillful way to pray outside our church and home.

Bringing silent, meditative prayer into our daily life means we have a more intimate contact with Jesus, God, Mary, and whichever of the Christian saints we have a connection with. If there is trouble in the workplace, at home, or any situation in which we have become embroiled, we can silently pray for wisdom and grace to deal with it calmly and skillfully. We can visualize Jesus standing near us, his face expressing love and compassion for all the people involved, however angry anyone may have become. Jesus's universal love can be a strong reminder to avoid getting caught up in negative behavior that will only cause further suffering. We can remember his calm compassion toward those who hurt him and draw strength from it.

we can turn to god in silent prayer to
help us find inner peace and patience
at any time; he will always hear us....god
listens to our thoughts as much as
our speech

Catholics and Greek Orthodox practitioners use prayer beads called rosaries, which can be used by anyone who prays. A rosary is a string of beads with gaps marked by larger beads to facilitate counting. At the end is a crucifix. We start by making the sign of the cross and then use the beads to count off repeated prayers, as many as we wish. A rosary can be worn around the wrist like a bracelet, so that it is accessible all the time. We can use our rosary for meditative prayer in any daily life situation, such as walking down the street, on the bus, or in the park. Praying like this helps us develop focus and patience through our devotion and brings a feeling of inner peace. In this way we feel closer to God and gain spiritual benefit from saying prayers.

During Catholic confession a certain number of prayers are given by the priest as penance, an expression of repentance. For example, he may tell the person confessing to say 10 Hail Marys and 5 Our Fathers to repent for some negative action. Confessing our misdemeanors to the priest and receiving his absolution can bring great peace of mind because we let go of our bad behavior and move forward. Reciting the prayers given by the priest is a formal repentance. Even if we are not Catholic, we can still use prayers in daily life to repent for some negative action. Quietly reciting prayers, contemplating the foolishness of the behavior, and resolving not to repeat it can be an effective way for all of us to express regret and then move on.

confessing our misdemeanors to the priest

and receiving his absolution can bring

great peace of mind because we let go of

our bad behavior and move forward

God reveals himself in nature, so silent meditative prayer in natural places can enhance our faith in God. We can find a tranquil, beautiful spot and enjoy the marvel of creation just by sitting quietly and appreciating the tranquillity, feeling the outer peace becoming inner peace. Great Christian poets such as John Donne, George Herbert, and William Wordsworth expressed their appreciation and wonder at God's creation through devotional poems on nature. These poems are like meditations and reveal a deep spiritual understanding. We can read one of these poems, silently or out loud, and share the joy and inspiration of the poet's closeness to God through nature.

christian mantra

There is a tradition of Christian mantra meditation that is simple, and yet the benefits are immense, according to various testimonies of saints and meditators. It is often assumed that only the Eastern religions use mantras, but the Christian monk Cassian, who lived during the fifth century, developed and used the same method of mantra in an authentic Christian context. The tradition originated from the Fathers of the Desert and was practiced for some time, but gradually became lost to all but a few. The tradition was renewed in the last century by the Benedictine monk John Main, who first encountered mantra through the great Hindu master Swami Satyananda in Malaya. When he stumbled across a similar but Christian mantra practice in a medieval treatise, he realized its potential not just for monastics but for all Christians and indeed for all people.

maranatha is an aramaic word

that means "come lord, come lord jesus."

we find this word in the bible,

used by st. paul at the end of his...

letter to the corinthians

John Main realized that this way of prayer was suitable for people in the modern world. The number of practicing Christians has declined substantially over the last few decades, partly because of practices and attitudes that bear little relevance to modern life. This rediscovery of Christian mantra that could be used by anyone gave a much needed injection of life to many practicing Christians and also attracted people who had not previously considered prayer relevant to daily life. Thanks to John's efforts the World Community for Christian Meditation was formed, and now has many thousands of members internationally.

Although the actual practice of reciting the mantra, sitting in the classic meditation posture, is similar to those from the Eastern traditions we have already looked at, the philosophy behind the practice is different and based very much in Christianity. In Cassian's writing, he suggests the idea of becoming "grandly poor" by restricting himself to one mantra only. He felt the simplicity of this helped gain a deeper understanding of Jesus' comment "Blessed are the poor in spirit." The idea of being faithful to one mantra also deepens the concept of faith.

The mantra that is recommended is a word that has been hallowed for centuries in the Christian tradition. The word is "maranatha" and is pronounced with equal stress on all four syllables. Maranatha is an Aramaic word that means "Come Lord, come Lord Jesus." We find this word in the Bible, used by St. Paul at the end of his famous first letter to the Corinthians and also by St. John at the end of the Book of Revelation. Thus the mantra is steeped in Christian faith, yet because it is Aramaic we do not have the same associations as we would were we to use the more familiar word "Jesus." This allows the meditation to remain pure and free from images.

the prayer of the heart

Christian prayer is a way of communicating with God. Many Christians also pray to try to bring about the experience of being filled with the Holy Spirit, as is also the case with repeating the mantra maranatha. The faithful repetition of the mantra deepens the awareness of the Spirit working within us, and we realize a sense of creative wholeness and harmony throughout our being. Eventually we become filled with "the peace that passeth all understanding," the all-pervasive peace of mind, body, and spirit. Though we say the mantra silently in our mind, this gradually expands until we arrive at a point where we feel it in our heart, what the Christian spiritual masters have called the "prayer of the heart." This removes the duality of mind and heart, which was believed to have caused the original fall from grace. By transcending this artificial duality, we feel united within ourselves with God and with everything in creation, ultimately reaching a state of grace.

though we say the mantra silently in our mind, this gradually expands until we arrive at a point where we feel it in our heart, what the christian spiritual masters have called the "prayer of the heart"

The best way to work with the mantra maranatha is to set aside 20 to 30 minutes twice a day to practice the meditation. Sit in the classic meditation posture and simply start repeating the mantra silently in your mind. Eventually the word will start to resonate throughout your being, but at the beginning it is important to simply repeat the word silently for the whole session. Mental distractions will inevitably arise, and you might discover you have stopped repeating the word. Simply return to the mantra if this happens. Try not to think or imagine anything during the practice; just repeat the mantra quietly with patience and faith.

Christian meditation leads us toward self-transcendence, beyond the duality of separation from God. Through our union with God we transcend ourselves, and enter the process of divine creation, the expression of God. Meditation itself is the process of self-transcendence, and leads us toward an experience of divinity, becoming one with the power of love. Thus each time we meditate our little individual self-transcendence helps the liberation of human consciousness, which is the ultimate meaning of God's creation.

zen and the arts

Zen Buddhism is brought into the realm of daily life by the practice of certain art forms or ceremonies, such as *ikebana*, or flower arranging, the famous tea ceremony, and the arts of calligraphy, dance, swordsmanship, and archery. In fact, from the viewpoint of Zen, the whole of life can be regarded as an art, and we try to live every moment in complete mindfulness in order to awaken to our true nature, the enlightened state. The contemporary American practitioner of Zen dance Sun Ock Lee describes the view of Zen thus: "Every human action may be undertaken as an exercise toward enlightenment and performed in such a way as to suggest the ineffable." In this way all of life becomes an art form, which we try to practice with mindfulness at all times.

The Zen arts are first and foremost meant to train the mind, and all utilitarian, aesthetic, and pleasurable functions are secondary. The mind must first be attuned to lack of self-consciousness to bring it into contact with ultimate reality before one undertakes any of these arts. Thus the tea ceremony is not solely for quenching thirst, the dancer does not just perform rhythmical movements of the body, and the swordsman does not wield his sword only to outplay his opponent. Technical knowledge alone is insufficient to become a master of any of the arts, so technique must be transcended and any residual sense of self dissolved into the activity itself.

the tea ceremony is not solely

for quenching thirst

The Zen teachings are notoriously difficult to elucidate. They are elusive by design because the second you think you have understood some aspect of Zen, the mind has grasped hold of it and then it is lost. This is demonstrated by koans, which are designed to break the usual conventional mode of thought to discover other ways to use the mind and thus cannot be understood in any conventional sense. Yet the essence of Zen is also simplicity and described by the great Zen masters as nothing more than "everyday mind." In this way we sleep when tired, eat when hungry, and so forth. However, the minute we think about sleeping and so on, the original mind is lost and we become caught up in reflections, deliberations, and conceptualizations. Then we are no longer eating purely; thought has interfered with the process, and the essence of Zen is gone. Practicing any of the Zen arts helps us find the childlike simplicity we have lost.

With the art of flower arranging, the master "becomes" the flowers and the vase, because there is no sense of an "I" doing anything. He or she slowly unties the bast or roll of cloth holding the flowers together, rolls it up, and carefully places it to one side. Then each spray of blossom is picked up and examined minutely before being bent into exactly the right shape and placed in the vase. The result is as perfect as nature intended and as exquisite as a picture. Zen masters efface themselves in the art of shaping and creating; the expressive power results from the master's mind and the flowers having become as one. There is only the immediate experience of the moment, which cannot be understood intellectually, and can be known only through not knowing.

each spray of blossom is picked up

and examined minutely

The ineffable truth of ultimate reality can only be directly experienced, not described, which is why the Zen texts remain cryptic and largely indecipherable unless the reader has tasted of the same truth. We can learn only by doing, by practicing any of these arts. Reading descriptions is like trying to understand the taste of chocolate cake by reading the instructions on how to bake it. Nonetheless we must start somewhere, and reading about something may stimulate the impulse to do it. We can also try things out for ourselves to discover whether this path to enlightenment suits our disposition before attempting the difficult task of finding a master to train us in one of the Zen arts.

practicing rituals

We can devise our own tea ceremony, bearing in mind the importance of using it as mindfulness training. The traditional tea ceremony emphasizes ritual as a technique to remain mindful and in each moment. We first select the most beautiful and graceful implements: teapot, cup, saucer, teaspoon, tray, sugar bowl, milk jug, and finest leaf tea. We prepare a place to sit that is quiet, refined, and suitable for drinking-tea meditation. It is sensible to have either a real or a mental picture of how the tea tray will look and then to place each implement precisely and mindfully. Every little action is performed with the same meditative grace. Try not to think about what you are doing. Try to lose the sense of self and be fully immersed in the ceremony. As you finally drink the tea, be aware of each tiny sensation you normally do not notice. Drink slowly and mindfully. When you finish try to keep the mindfulness as you go about your daily life.

Zen calligraphy works in quite a different way from both flower arranging and tea ceremony. Here mindfulness is combined with spontaneity. The Zen

master sits quietly with paper, brush, and ink laid out close by. During this meditation he or she examines the brush, prepares the ink, smooths and straightens the paper. Suddenly the master seizes the brush and swiftly paints a syllable, trying to be like a flash of lightning from the cloud of all-encompassing truth in the spontaneous free movement of spirit that paints the character. Many are discarded because they are confused, meaning contrived in some way, though to the untrained eye the difference is imperceptible. Finally the master paints a syllable that he or she knows is harmonious, perfect in the moment of execution with no sense of self, simply the spontaneous act of painting the character.

In Zen archery there is no point in aiming for anything except oneself, a cryptic way of saying that the archer finds him- or herself only by losing the sense of self in the art of drawing the bow and loosing the arrow. Letting go of any idea of archer and shot, the master draws the bow slowly toward the point of highest tension in the most relaxed way possible. The shot eventually "falls" from the bow and strikes the target effortlessly. A Zen master archer describes the process thus:

"You can learn from an ordinary
bamboo leaf what ought to happen.
It bends lower and lower under the
weight of snow. Suddenly the snow slips
to the ground without the leaf
having stirred. Stay like that at the
point of highest tension until the
shot falls from you. So, indeed it is;
when the tension is fulfilled, the shot
must fall, it must fall from the archer
like snow from a bamboo leaf, before
he even thinks it."

In this way the archer meets both his original essence and the all-encompassing truth of ultimate reality; he realizes they are one and the same and stares enlightenment in the face.

All of the Zen arts take many years of training both in technique and in mindfulness in order to arrive at utmost simplicity of enlightenment. Mastering the various techniques is not to be underestimated. Each technique must be fully learned before a true understanding arises spontaneously that it must also be let go. Let's look to Zen swordsmanship. The new student arrives fearless and full of confidence from sword fighting in battle. As he learns the technique of swordsmanship in detail, he realizes how much he does not know and lives in fear of the more nimble and experienced opponent. After diligent practice he becomes brilliant at the technique and his self-confidence is restored. But now he must learn from the master to be purposeless, egoless, and detached. Only then will he truly have learned Zen swordsmanship and be able to win effortlessly, because he has gone beyond any idea of winning.

jewish prayer

Prayer is a private communion between an individual and God. In Judaism private prayer may supplement communal prayers in the synagogue, which are believed to incorporate a deeper level of spirituality. The Divine Presence, or Shekhinah, manifests with the assembly of the faithful, which is defined as a quorum (*minyan*) of 10 male Jews over the age of 13. The Talmud assigns women to the private sphere of the home and they do not make up the prayer quorum. However, the Talmud records at least one instance when a woman's prayer is superior to that of her husband, and non-Orthodox branches of Judaism have more or less given women equality of status with men in the synagogue.

the essence of prayer

The Talmudic rabbis introduced the idea of inwardness or *kavvannah*, meaning literally intention or direction. This arose from the study of Hannah's prayer for a child, which was seen to demonstrate an inner commitment of the heart, rather than just a simple reciting of the words. This is now regarded as the essence of prayer, to recite the words meaningfully together with a profound sense of awe and mystery. Mindfulness is further encouraged by reciting B'rakhot (singular B'rakhah) or blessings, and observant Jews recite 100 a day before and after many daily life activities. The Zohar, the 13th-century Spanish Kabbalah, took this idea of meaningful prayer even further by describing it as a Jacob's ladder uniting earth and heaven, man and God.

The Hebrew term for prayer is *tefillah*, which is derived from a word meaning to judge or self-examine, implying introspection and a modifying of the one who prays. In this way, we gain spiritual development through prayer and arrive at a better understanding of ourselves. Prayer ideally is combined with studying and learning the Torah and the performance of deeds of loving-kindness, which Judaism demands.

There are three daily orders of service practiced by devout Jews, consisting of Maariv (or Arvit) in the evening, Shacharit in the morning, and Minchah in the afternoon. On the Sabbath there is an additional service, Musaf, which follows Shacharit. Two major prayers are recited during these services. The Shema consists of three scriptural readings and commences with the declaration of God's unity; it is recited at Maariv and Shacharit but not at Minchah. The Amidah (also known as the Shemoneh Esreh, which means 18, the original number of paragraphs in the prayer) consists of praise, petitions to God, and thanksgiving, and is recited at all three services. However, petitions to God are not included on the Sabbath, God's day of rest.

"Hear, O Israel! The Lord is our God.
The Lord is One! Blessed be his name,
whose glorious kingdom is for ever and
ever. And you shall love the Lord your
God with all your heart, with all your
soul, and with all your strength. And
these words which I command you today,
shall be upon your heart. And you shall
teach them to your children, and speak
of them, when you sit in your house,
when you walk by the way, and when
you lie down and when you rise."

Extract from the Shema

Each prayer must be said in the appropriate attitude. The Amidah is recited quietly, standing in a reverential position with the feet together and facing in the direction of Jerusalem. At four particular points in the prayer one performs a small bow. The Shema is recited in whatever position one feels is appropriately devotional. But when you commit yourself to the unity of God in the first verse, you should close your eyes and cover them with your hands in intense concentration.

There are also prayers and rituals to be performed in the home, such as the woman of the house lighting candles on the eve of the Sabbath, and the man of the house saying Kiddush before partaking of the Sabbath meal. Kiddush is a sanctification of time, an act of making the day holy, and a blessing, traditionally said over a glass of wine as a blessing for the day. Every aspect of life is considered a vehicle for devotion to God, and true spirituality is found in the home and in social relationships as much as in prayer, learning, and the various ascetic practices, such as fasting. Judaism thus honors formal, traditional prayer and encourages prayer and spirituality to be a part of daily life.

islamic prayer

The familiar *al-hamdu lillah*, meaning "praise be to God," and *in sha Allah*, meaning "if God is willing," are oft-quoted Koranic phrases that show how far these scriptures have penetrated into the everyday language of people from many religions and cultures, not just Muslims. "Praise be to God" is the acknowledgment that the credit for everything that happens belongs to God, and "if God is willing" is an expression of deference to God's omnipotence and grace in all future events. Though in common parlance these phrases tend to be used as a kind of superstitious mantra to ward off misfortune, they nonetheless ground the speaker in a belief, albeit often unconsciously, in the omnipresence of God.

Perhaps another reason for the familiarity of these phrases is the sheer number of Islamic communities and the fact that they are almost without exception devout practitioners, whether fundamentalist or not. It is estimated that today the number of Muslims across the world is substantially more than a billion, or approximately one-fifth of the world's population.

Muslim communities are not found solely in what we would describe as traditional Muslim countries. There are many different Muslim communities spread throughout the Western world. All Muslims are united in their scripture, the Koran, and daily devotional recitation at set times forms the basis of Islamic prayer.

the five daily prayers

The haunting cry of the muezzin, the official of the mosque, calling the faithful to pray from atop the minaret, is a beautiful and unforgettable sound heard throughout the day in Muslim countries. The faithful undertake the five obligatory daily prayers, starting at dawn, and these can be performed either alone or within a congregation. The prayers consist of sections called *rak'as* which are repeated either twice or four times. Each *rak'a* is accompanied by bows and prostrations, though the raising of the hands prior to prostrating is performed only by males.

The prayers consist of reciting parts of the Koran, and prayers always commence with the recitation of the Fatiha, the opening verse of the Koran. This is followed by a further recitation in which the worshipper has some free choice in the verses to recite. These can be quite minimal or as long as desired but must fulfill the criteria of either a minimum of three short verses or a complete *sura*, or chapter. In practice these are often short, as can be seen by the following example, which incidentally is both three short verses and a complete *sura*. Brevity is useful because prayers are never read directly from the holy book itself, but are only ever recited from memory.

> *"he is god, one god, the everlasting refuge,*
>
> *who has not begotten, and has not been*
>
> *begotten, and equal to him is not anyone"*

Extract from the Koran

Formal recitation of the Koran, either parts of it or the entire text, is undertaken either by very devout individuals as they go about their daily life or by trained reciters. In early 19th-century Egypt, for example, it was common "entertainment" at parties to have three or four experienced reciters, who during the course of the party would recite between them the whole of the Koran. This would take about nine hours but guests were free to take breaks and were not expected to listen faithfully the entire time. However, the reciters were highly trained to recite in moving and almost musical tones that were often exquisite as well as spiritual so that many guests listened to much of the recital.

integrating prayer into daily life

Informal recitation of the Koran is a real integration of prayer into daily life, as we saw from the familiarity of the two common phrases. The Koran is turned to often in times of crisis. For example, when a child is ill the parents sit beside the sickbed, reciting verses from the Koran for hours at a time. This frequent recitation from the Koran both in formal prayer and in daily life permeates all of life with scriptural references, which is perhaps difficult for non-Muslims to comprehend. However, the constant reminders of God's presence in this way can bring extraordinary spiritual riches into ordinary life.

Of all the world's major religions, Islam is perhaps the least affected by the modern malaise of irreligion. The questioning of spiritual authority has a largely scientific basis, and because religious truth cannot be demonstrated to be "true" using scientific criteria, it is often dismissed as superstitious, outdated nonsense. Modern science is perceived as a mainly Western invention, and from the fundamentalist Muslim perspective is sometimes regarded as part of the evils of the Western world. The fundamentalists have been at the forefront of Islamic culture and have kept the religion sacrosanct. Although fundamentalism has certain drawbacks, nonetheless Islam has been preserved relatively unchanged for centuries.

meditation centers
and organizations

Buddhist Meditation

Gaia House, West Ogwell, Newton Abbot, Devon TQ12 6EN, UK

Insight Meditation Society

Pleasant Street, Barre, MA 01005, USA

Sharpham College of Buddhist Studies & Contemporary Enquiry

Sharpham House, Ashprington, Totnes, Devon TQ9 7UT, UK

The World Community for Christian Meditation

23 Kensington Square, London W8 5HN, UK

The World Community for Christian Meditation

The John Main Institute, 7315 Brookville Road, Chevy Chase, MD 20815, USA

Kanzeon Sangha – Zen Practice Centre Trust

26 Salisbury Road, Maidstone, Kent ME14 2TX, UK

The Sufi Order

SufiOrder@compuserve.com

UK Islamic Academy

147 Mere Road, Leicester LE5 5GQ, UK

Web sites

www.chanmyay.net: network of Buddhist meditation centers worldwide

www.retreatsonline.com: worldwide information on spiritual retreats

www.whiteeaglelodge.com: worldwide information on meditation, healing, and retreats

glossary

aramaic: a Semitic language commonly spoken when Jesus was alive

asana: yoga position, usually taken up and held for some time

atman: divine, absolute being in Hinduism

buddhanature: the potential within all living beings to become a buddha

bindus: tiny drops of subtle energy

bija: literally, seed-syllable

chakras: energy centers in the body's subtle energy system

channels/meridians/*nadis*: pathways along which subtle energy travels

chi: subtle energy

dharma: the teachings of the Buddha

drops: *see bindus*

guru: eastern spiritual teacher or guide

lokas: realms of existence

mandala: a graphic representation of both the Buddhist cosmos and the human being

mantra: a short phrase of sacred syllables chanted like a prayer

meridians: *see* channels

nadi: *see* channels

pali: an Indo-Aryan language used to first write the Buddha's words after his death

prana: subtle energy

saddhu: Indian holy man

samatha: calm meditation

sangha: spiritual community in Buddhism, often referring to monastics

sanskrit: ancient Indian classical language used for writing scriptures

sefirot (singular sefirah): holy spheres on the Kabbalistic Tree of Life

shinto: ancient Japanese folk religion

stupa: reliquary holding sacred relics of the Buddha or Buddhist saints

subtle energy: *see* chi

sutra **or** *sutta*: the teachings of the Buddha

talmud: the compilation of ancient Jewish law and tradition

vipassana: insight meditation

winds: subtle energy that moves in the channels

yin yang circle: ancient Taoist symbol reflecting how opposites move into each other

zafu: meditation cushion

index

bibliography
and acknowledgments

I would like to thank everyone who helped with this book, including all those involved at Mitchell Beazley and my agent and good friend, Liz Puttick. I am indebted to all my fellow seekers on various spiritual paths who have been so generous with their advice and knowledge. Special thanks to my partner, Robert Beer, for his love, wisdom, and patient support throughout the writing of this book.

Basho, Matsuo **The Narrow Road to the Deep North** London, Penguin Books, 1966

Batchelor, Martine **Walking on Lotus Flowers** London, Harper Collins/Thorsons, 1996

Batchelor, Stephen **The Awakening of the West** London, Harper Collins/Aquarian, 1994

Batchelor, Stephen **Buddhism Without Beliefs** New York, Riverhead Books, 1997

Beer, Robert **The Encyclopedia of Tibetan Symbols & Motifs** London, Serindia Publications, 1999

Berg, Michael **The Way: Using the Wisdom of Kabbalah for Spiritual Transformation and Fulfillment** New York, John Wiley & Sons, 2001

Cade, C. Maxwell and Coxhead, Nona **The Awakened Mind** Middlesex, Wildwood House, 1983

Cook, Michael **The Koran: A Very Short Introduction** Oxford, Oxford University Press, 2000

Crocker, Richard **An Introduction to Gregorian Chant** New Haven and London, Yale University Press, 2000

Farrer-Halls, Gill **The Illustrated Encyclopedia of Buddhist Wisdom** New Alresford, Godsfield Press, 2000

Farrer-Halls, Gill **Meditations & Rituals Using Aromatherapy Oils** New Alresford, Godsfield Press, 2001

Farrer-Halls, Gill **The World of the Dalai Lama** London, Harper Collins/Thorsons, 1998

Feuerstein, Georg **Encyclopedic Dictionary of Yoga** London, Unwin Hyman, 1990

Feuerstein, Georg and Bodian, Stephan **Living Yoga: A Comprehensive Guide for Daily Life** Los Angeles, Jeremy P. Tarcher, 1993

Fortune, Dion **The Mystical Qabalah** London, Harper Collins/Aquarian, 1987

Herrigel, Eugen **Zen in the Art of Archery** London, Penguin/Arkana, 1985

Hittleman, Richard **Yoga for Total Fitness** New York, Bantam Books, 1983

Kabat-Zinn **Mindfulness Meditation: Cultivating the Wisdom of Your Body and Mind** New York, Simon & Schuster, 1995

Kabat-Zinn **Wherever You Go, There You Are: Mindfulness Meditation in Everyday Life** New York, Hyperion, 1995

Khan, Pir Vilayat Inayat **Thinking Like the Universe: the Sufi Path of Awakening** London, Harper Collins/Thorsons, 2000

Liu, Da **T'ai Chi Ch'uan & I Ching** London & Henley, Routledge & Kegan Paul, 1985

McDonald, Kathleen **How to Meditate** Massachussetts, Wisdom Publications, 1984

Main, John **The Inner Christ** London, Darton, Longman & Todd, 1999

Scholem, Gershom **Kabbalah** London, Penguin, 1978

Snelling, John **The Buddhist Handbook** London, Rider, 1998

Solomon, Norman **Judaism: A Very Short Introduction** Oxford, Oxford University Press, 1996

Suzuki, Daisetz Teitaro **An Introduction to Zen Buddhism** London, Rider, 1991

Titmuss, Christopher **The Power of Meditation** London, The Apple Press, 1999